Too Clever By Half
a fair deal for gifted children

Too Clever By Half
a fair deal for gifted children

Carrie Winstanley

Trentham Books

Stoke on Trent, UK and Sterling, USA

Trentham Books Limited

Westview House	22883 Quicksilver Drive
734 London Road	Sterling
Oakhill	VA 20166-2012
Stoke on Trent	USA
Staffordshire	
England ST4 5NP	

© 2004 Carrie Winstanley

First published 2004

British Library Cataloguing-in-Publication Data
A catalogue record for this book is available from the British Library

1 85856 327 5

Cover photograph: Suzi Winstanley

Designed and typeset by Trentham Print Design Ltd., Chester and printed in Great Britain by Alden Group Ltd., Oxford.

Contents

Acknowledgements

To Ma, Pa and Suzi

My motivation for writing this book comes directly from the children I have worked with over the years. Some of them feature at the start of a chapter. Their experiences and comments have been playing in my mind and sometimes when I was writing I would picture their faces and try to answer their questions.

My wonderful family have been unswervingly understanding and patient. Ma was my first teaching role model and inspiration and Pa, Suzi and Missy have helped me keep going whilst keeping it all in perspective. Thanks to Gilberto and Damon for help along the way. Danny has been a brilliant teaching partner, reliable life-saver and an uncanny mind-reader.

Heartfelt thanks to friends Jo, Gilsemar, Jacque and Miki, Michael, Dianne and Mike Flynn for tea, sympathy and practical help, and to the Basketball Crew for keeping me on my toes. Roehampton has helped with financial aid, time, support and encouragement, and dear colleagues Roger Marples and Ron Best have been immensely accommodating. I have many other people to thank for support and encouragement, such as the GIFT staff, teachers and the children so willing to share ideas, adventures and opinions at numerous workshops.

I have been privileged to work with generous and supportive Professors John White and Harry Brighouse and to be part of a lively philosophy department with stimulating and committed staff and students. The opportunity to present and discuss my work has been a vital part of my development.

I am very grateful to Gillian for suggesting this project (and for the swimming) and also to John at Trentham for getting excited about the important things.

Thanks.

Introduction

Ideal children: André , Doris, both age 8, Year 4

These children were both all-rounders; good at pretty much every subject, and able to demonstrate outstanding achievement in some. Both excelled in maths and English, humanities and general science. Doris was an accomplished musician and dancer and André was a splendid cricketer and the computing expert teachers called on when the lab crashed. Doris was the more out-going, but both had many firm friends and were liked by teachers, auxiliary staff and parents. They were both star pupils but neither had let success go to their heads. Contrary to the stereotype, they were sociable, capable, helpful, humble and friendly. In short, they were model pupils.

Do you think you're good at learning?

André: Not at everything like English and French. I am at Maths, though I think it's hard work too. People say I'm a lucky beggar, but I do have to work as well. I like to do as well as I can.

Doris: I can learn dances really quickly. It's my talent and so I have to use it every day. I can't learn maths so well because it's too hard to bother with. I prefer other things. I think I'm good at learning things I like. Maybe I like things I'm good at learning. I've never really thought about it. That's a good one. I'll think about this later.

What this book is about

André and Doris are the exception amongst gifted children rather than the rule. Enjoying school and achieving in line with their high ability, they typify the children people have in mind when they dismiss extra resources and activities as unnecessary for the gifted. In this book I show that there are many different types of highly able children and that they all merit appropriate challenge even where this implies increased resources or a change in the structures of schooling.

Case studies and examples

Each chapter begins with illustrative case studies of children with whom I have worked, so demonstrating the diversity of high ability. All the children in these case studies had been identified as highly able from more than one source (eg. another teacher's nomination and psychologist's report). All names have been changed. What they say here is in answer to the question 'Do you think you're good at learning?' Throughout the book are other examples of incidents from my own teaching experience in a range of diverse settings.

How I came to this area

There can be a palpable sense of disapproval and even hostility when I explain to people that I work with highly able children. It is not politically correct. Many of the arguments against provision for the able are based on misunderstandings about the field and scant knowledge about able pupils, however. The field of gifted education has contributed to its own difficulties, though, as we will see.

Like many academics who research into high ability, my background falls within the discipline of psychology and work in schools as a teacher and special educational needs coordinator (Senco). I found the underpinning assumptions of the psychological constructs lacked rigorous examination, often ignoring the complex ethical arguments in which gifted education is unwillingly immersed, and my search for a more analytical approach led me to philosophy of education.

I have continued to work in a range of settings and a variety of roles including mainstream classrooms, an independent school for the gifted, as a Senco, at museum and school workshops and in weekend and holiday schemes. I have delivered in-service education for teachers and worked with students, affording me opportunities to work with practitioners. So I have had access to a broad spectrum of views and working styles.

The structure of the book

The overwhelming assumption for detractors of gifted education is that those who work in the field are supporting elitism and exclusivity in education. Some teachers would be happy with these reasons for provision, but they are a minority (Delisle, 1994a, 1994b). It is difficult to articulate why the highly able merit support, but I take a fresh look at key issues and present coherent arguments that tackle the contentious aspects. These fall into three areas: the nature of high ability; fairness of provision; and the nature of provision.

The book is interdisciplinary, drawing on philosophy, psychology, gifted education and practice to answer the key question of how we can provide for the highly able. The first part of the book asks 'Who are the highly able?' It has two chapters:

1 *The language of high ability*
2 *Who are the highly able?*

These chapters consider the language needed for this discussion and focus on defining the target group. This is useful for teachers and policy makers as it clarifies who counts as able and also demonstrates where problems lie in the literature. The second part of the book presents an ethical argument in favour of provision for the target group, addressing the question 'Why should we make provision for the highly able?' This section has three chapters that show why highly able children are entitled to provision and provides compelling reasons for provision while showing the problems with commonly expressed arguments:

3 *The case for making provision*
4 *Arguments for and against provision for the highly able*
5 *Equality of challenge*

The last part of the book looks at practical responses to the needs of the highly able. Three chapters consider what we should do for highly able children, through general provision, critical thinking skills programmes and finally Philosophy with Children:

The conclusion summarises implications for further research and for teachers and policy makers.

Putting the book into context: global concerns

High ability is an issue of worldwide concern, but since no education system operates in a vacuum, invasive political issues and extant value systems must be taken into consideration by policy makers, teachers and researchers. Effective communication between researchers from different countries would reduce the wheel reinvention that characterises the field of gifted education. Despite countries' varied economic, political and value systems, there are notable similarities.

> Common to all nations, presumably, are abilities, which deviate from the accepted norms by level or nature. Many of the problems encountered by implementing Gifted Education worldwide are likely to be the same rather than unique, or at least related, on social-psychological grounds. *Persson, Joswig and Balogh, 2000:726*

The UK Gifted and Talented government strategy is comparatively new (1999) and teachers would be forgiven for thinking that this reflects global development in this field. Even a cursory glance at the research, however, indicates that the debates just beginning to intensify in the UK have been raging for decades elsewhere. A central theme of discussions, found in varying degrees and different guises around the world, is the apparent conflict between aims of excellence and of equality.

Even though the international picture is fractured and scattered, common issues have been debated and examined in a way that can improve practice. Learning from others' experiences can help us better understand how children are being hampered and how they can be helped to flourish, and this will help facilitate positive developments for the future of gifted education

> Policies on educating gifted students worldwide are generally traditional in their definitions of giftedness and models of pro-

viding accommodations for those students in school settings ... new models that reflect the needs of a global, information society and economy are needed. Talent development models and international models are the first step toward meeting the needs of the 21st century. *Rudnitski, 2000:678*

An overview of international research demonstrates the complexities of both definition and provision. It also shows how high ability must be considered in terms of local social contexts if practical solutions to potential problems are to be found.

Putting the book into context: the intractable problem of defining the highly able

To cater effectively for the able, objective, clear and agreed criteria of high ability are needed, on which teachers can build a framework for support. However, determining these causes disagreement within individual schools, as well as in national and international contexts. Consequently, the task of definition occupies much literature and research, typified by these observations from Eyre (1997):

> Identification is without doubt an important but also troublesome area in the education of able pupils, ... the key messages are:
>
> definition and identification are closely linked;
> testing alone cannot provide the answer;
> able pupils are not a clearly defined group;
> some abilities may not be recognised until later in a pupil's schooling;
> ability and achievement are not the same thing; opportunities and motivation make a difference. (p35-6)
>
> Effective identification procedures are usually extensive and permeate all aspects of the school structure. They are not a 'bolt-on' activity. (p24)

Multiple definitions and myriad checklists exist. Researchers have identified characteristics common to many able pupils, in the hope that ticking off certain behaviours and attitudes rather than just looking at achievement, would help assign pupils for provision. Unfortunately, in aiming for an inclusive approach, lists become unwieldy, ranging too widely to be useful, sometimes with contradictory indications:

able pupils are likely to:

demonstrate unusual curiosity	exhibit boredom;
finish work with ease and speed	take extra time to complete tasks to a high standard;
have many friends	be quite isolated;
contribute willingly in class	refuse to comply with instructions;
be interested in a broad variety of topics	only express interest in a narrow range of subjects

... etc ...

These examples are taken from the DfES website *Excellence in Cities* (2002) and from Eyre (1997). Both sources used these indicators, scattered throughout the website or book.

> Nowadays, a look through the relevant literature pertaining to giftedness research can be quite confusing due to the amazing variety of definitions for giftedness or gifted persons. *Ziegler and Heller, 2000:6*

The group of pupils who count as able should also, therefore, involve potentially able children. But this creates a large cohort that is more difficult to recognise and which will have diverse needs.

> ...the task of identification shifts from a search for the gifted few to assessment of the talent, strengths and aptitudes of all students, and to identification of high level talent potential among those who are especially precocious or advanced in their talent development. ...it is becoming clear that relatively large numbers of youth demonstrate one or more potential talent strengths ... which if identified and nurtured may lead to high level creative achievement in adulthood. *Feldhusen and Jarwan, 2000:279*

Outside of the field, the highly able are treated very much as a homogeneous group, but in the literature, heterogeneity is emphasised, as shown by this typical passage:

> It is important to realise that gifted and talented students are not a homogeneous group. They do not exhibit the same traits or characteristics, but rather a wide range of individual dif-

ferences. No single trait itself constitutes giftedness. Gifted and talented students often exhibit superior abilities and task commitment, not necessarily in pro-social ways or within the school curriculum. *George, 1992:16*

Commonly there is a notion of a spectrum of ability, with the highly able at one end and children with problems such as learning difficulties and disabilities at the other. Even teachers and psychologists tend to muddle low ability with learning problems but this is a false dichotomy and an over-simplification. Some children are able but have emotional troubles, learning problems or other difficulties. There is no merit in treating these pupils as a homogeneous group and putting them with able high achievers. Good practice entails careful consideration of the complex needs and entitlements; practice that takes account of children's differences.

Most education professionals would agree that support for pupils with difficulties should be matched to their areas of strength as well as their weaknesses. Helping them can be difficult when it is not clear how they can be defined and recognised. Possible explanations for missing such able children and for false positives include:

May appear able if:	*May be missed if:*
speaks confidently	English is the second language
mature	quiet
reads early	poor physical coordination
good motor skills	slow to read and write
born Sept/Dec	summer birthday
good general knowledge	little pre-school experience
has bright siblings	has slow siblings
attractive and lively	scruffy and unappealing

Eyre, 1997:30

Teachers do not have much of a forum for issues of high ability, and in training competing pressures have compromised discussion time. This can mean that newly qualified teachers have limited experience of the highly able, and little time for considering their nature and needs. In light of the difficulties identifying and providing for the highly able, this could cause problems. In my contact with educators, I find deep interest in relevant debate but it is often accompanied by conceptual confusion and a focus only on the origins of abilities, rather than the nature of appropriate provision.

This book focuses on how best to nurture abilities. All of us have talents and aptitudes, but they are in different areas and at different levels. This does not make some people more valuable than others, merely better than others at doing x or y. When appreciating a broad range of abilities and allowing people to work on them, further skills and aptitudes could be revealed. I explore how we can foster and develop abilities, using a definition that is inclusive of many, rather than exclusive and narrow.

Putting the book into context: the underachieving able child

This book has a particular slant towards a sub-group of highly able pupils – underachieving able pupils. Such pupils have been somewhat neglected in research, literature and policy making, and misunderstood in school. In my experience, these pupils are often mistakenly rated as less able by their teachers, who find it difficult to accept that children can be able and still having learning and other problems. Not only do the highly able not constitute a single, homogeneous group, but their underachievement can have many causes. These include emotional problems, learning difficulties and disabilities.

High ability amongst children is generally associated with the five-year-old musical prodigy, the teenager with outstanding examination results or the international gymnast. Certainly, the able pupil in school is most often described through their consistently high grades and extra-curricular accomplishments. Unsurprisingly, it is assumed that a pupil with average to poor performance is not particularly able, so their ability is often ignored. It is important to understand that achievement and ability are not always equally matched, and although most teachers would prefer to investigate pupils before leaping to any conclusion about their ability, this is not always possible. Unfortunately, when thorough examination of pupils is too time consuming for busy teachers, and reasons for weak school work are obscure, pupils can be presumed incapable at an early stage, a label that can be hard to shake off.

One possible explanation for underachievement is the interesting contradiction of 'dual exceptionality': when high ability is accompanied by some kind of a problem.

From observation, it seems dual exceptionalities are more common than most educators may think. ... Dual exceptionalities require a 'team' approach. School psychologists are in the best position to test and diagnose exceptionalities while the school counsellor (and at times school social worker) has the expertise for counselling the student and family regarding the dual exceptionalities. *Colangelo and Assouline, 2000:605*

These dual exceptionalities may take the form of sensory impairment, physical disability, learning difficulties, social, cultural or economic disadvantage. All can potentially cause underachievement

Putting the book into context:
provision for the able affects all pupils

Broadening the definition of high ability has made provision relevant to more pupils, partly through practical activities and partly through the changes in how we think about ability and intelligence.

Researchers now ask what kind of ability constitutes giftedness, how these abilities are organised and how they interact. Traditional tests of cognitive ability are being used to define patterns rather than levels, and there is an increasing interest in and emphasis upon cognitive structures and processes. The analysis and development of metacognitive abilities, problem solving and non-cognitive aspects, such as motivation, values and attitudes, self-image, confidence and dedication, social abilities and values, are some of the more recent and most important areas of investigation and development in identification of the able. *Montgomery, 1996:27*

Although they seem contradictory, excellence and equity are both vital concerns in gifted education as well as in broader education systems. Anything that can help resolve the conflicts between the two principles will also have an impact on the broader population of children in education.

The adoption of a simultaneous commitment toward excellence and equity in our schools holds promise for all participants within the learning community. Inclusive education offers the context for this to happen in general classrooms throughout the world, and eventually should figure strongly in helping to eliminate many of the limitations and barriers created out of separate, dual systems of regular and general education. *Yewchuk and Lupart, 2000:666*

Issues concerning the gifted field have never been confined to a small group of children and youth identified as 'gifted or talented' but have an impact on the whole of education. For example, the issues surrounding questions of *excellence and equity* affect all educational decisions [and] not just provision made for the gifted. Despite a century of programming for the gifted, such efforts are still debated as to whether they are elitist, undemocratic and even necessary. *Monks, Heller and Passow, 2000:839*

Gifted education is increasingly identified as a useful tool in helping disadvantaged pupils, since addressing the disadvantaged able highlights unfairness and removes barriers to success. Arguments for provision for the able are strengthened as a result.

There are five major social barriers, which, to a greater or lesser extent, exist everywhere in the world – political and social attitudes, poverty, gender, social disapproval and handicap (sic) – they were all present in this study. *Freeman, 2001:2*

If schools are not systematic and proactive in recognising ability and providing appropriate support, then pupils from disadvantaged backgrounds will be penalised and the children of white middle-class parents withdrawn from the state sector. Recognising able pupils is not an optional extra; it is an essential aspect of providing for good, comprehensive education. *1997:12*

Conclusion

In my work with able pupils, I have seen the problems faced by teachers, families and the pupils themselves at first hand, and want to highlight their difficulties and suggest some possible remedies.

To continue with the investigation, what is needed is a clear and coherent account of high ability to guide practice and policy making. Chapter 1 surveys the definitions used in literature and policy documents evaluating their worth.

PART ONE
Who are the highly able?

1

What's in a name?
The language of high ability

A frustrating pupil: Nat, age 14, Year 9

'Lazy' was the word most often used to describe Nat. He would not participate in anything much but demonstrated his ability by his accomplishment in school exams. Teachers would berate him for failing to attend class, emphasising the need to follow the curriculum and complete homework. He would defy and infuriate his teachers, excelling in tests and proving them wrong, reinforcing his contempt for school and irritating his less able and hard working peers. When compiling the school register for the able, staff argued over whether Nat should be included. His erratic performance was considered negative, but more than this, even though teachers agreed he made some startling contributions, his lack of effort made him 'unworthy' of inclusion alongside hardworking peers.

When Nat undertook his GCSEs the problems intensified. He refused to complete coursework until the last possible moment and then submitted weak and sketchy responses to set tasks, well below his obvious capabilities. Nat seemed to delight in annoying staff and appeared unperturbed at the prospect of leaving school with qualifications that did not reflect his ability.

Do you think you're good at learning?

Nat: [In a mock teacher tone] Well, what do you *mean* by learning? ... I know lots of things but I've known them for ages, I kind of got

3

the learning rather than doing it. You know, you read something roughly, but the details aren't helpful and you know what it's about without reading it all, anyway. Is that what you mean? You know what the teachers here think of me. That's why I'm here with you doing special needs; because I'm crap at learning. We all know I can't be bothered; I get out of lessons, you write in your folder or tape it all and there's no other ideas to make me care anyway. [As an aside] Is that the kind of thing you need for your folder, or do you want a bit more? You know, the peer pressure or home arguing-with-my-sister-stress or teenage hormone stuff. I could do an eating disorder for you if you want something more dramatic, but no psychology 'do these puzzle tests', OK?'

This chapter explores the language of high ability. It is both controversial and complex. Practitioners and policy makers use a wide range of different definitions of high ability, but we need a unified account, or at least more clarity in the debate. I survey the definitions most commonly found in literature and policy documents, and show where they are problematic, and in the following chapter I present my own understanding of high ability. Meanwhile, the word 'intelligence' is used in the dictionary definition sense: 'the capacity for understanding, ability to perceive and comprehend meaning' (Collins Dictionary, 1999:798).

As this is an interdisciplinary topic, I have focused on the definitions most likely to be accessed and used by teachers, rather than more strictly psychological or philosophical understandings. The aim is to explore the way in which highly able children are categorised, identified and discussed and to highlight the problems that arise from a lack of consensus in the material for practitioners and in the research.

It might (even) be said that, as in other fields, the more that is known, the more issues are raised and controversies are fuelled. ... Many different decisions regarding identification, education and counselling, for example, depend on the often only implicit conception and definition of giftedness. Therefore clarification of underlying constructs is essential for both program and research design. *Monks, Heller and Passow, 2000: 839 and 843*

Relevant literature is largely concerned with children, although significant longitudinal surveys have yielded interesting results, and there is a growing number of studies about young people[1] and adults with 'genius' status, some of whom are autistic savants and similar. (Although genius may seem removed from classroom issues, interesting studies could inform general pedagogic practice and shed light on whether some children learn in ways so removed from the average child that separate provision is unavoidable (see Yewchuck and Lupart, 1975 and Simonton, 2000).

I highlight the key issues that relate to concepts of high ability and the first task is to consider commonly adopted definitions partly through reviewing the enormous range found in the literature.

The Department for Education and Skills (DfES)

The Excellence in Cities (EiC) project is funded by the DfES and encompasses a Gifted and Talented strategy.[2] Like the QCA, the DfES is a government department with influence and substantial funding, so surely they will be clear about defining targeted pupils. In guidance on identifying the 'gifted and talented', the word 'able' is used without any explanation. 'Gifted' is never used, despite it being part of the title of the strategy.

> Schools can determine the proportion within the cohort of pupils with academic ability (defined as ability in one or more subjects in the statutory school curriculum other than art, music and PE), pupils with talent (defined as those with ability in art, music, PE, or in any sport or creative art) and 'all-rounders'. However, those with academic ability, including 'all-rounders', should form at least two-thirds of the cohort in each year group.
> *DfES website, March 2003*

The document continues in similar vein, giving practical advice but no clear definitions, underpinning theory, or reasoning. Current policy suggests that the top five to ten per cent of pupils should be classified as 'gifted and talented', but at termly Standing DfES conferences, this is always hotly contested, generating useful debate but seldom any conclusion.[3] Ofsted reports echo the concern over identifying the able, noting:

> The identification of gifted and talented pupils has presented difficulties for schools. To date, the methods of identification

have been rudimentary and have not yet solved the problem of recognising latent high ability, particularly among pupils who are underachieving generally. *Ofsted, 2001:3*

The first 'issue of attention' on the Ofsted list is to 'improve methods for identifying gifted and talented pupils', but no strategies for improving teacher understanding are presented and confusion seems set to continue. It would help practitioners to have access to an objective review of the literature to support the use of language and labels advocated by government departments responsible for making policy and building strategy (Ward, 2003).

Definitions

What, then, do researchers say? Practitioners need a clear definition of high ability to cater effectively for individual needs, but the area is a minefield. Ultimately, it may be impossible to find a definitive way of describing the able. Most writers develop a working definition, skating over underlying issues. That is a reasonable, practical approach. But is there a definitive description of high ability (Howe, 1990a, 1990b)?

The myriad of definitions is alarming. David George identifies 213 different definitions (1992:9) and observes that the heterogeneity of high ability makes 'vagueness a logical necessity'. Joan Freeman identifies 'more than 100', even within the relatively narrow foci of psychological constructs and academic success. Including other qualities, such as 'social talents and potential business acumen' would create a more complete picture but increase the number of definitions (1998:4). Broader definitions have appeared in UK accounts, and the search continues for yet more categories. A more inclusive definition would be welcomed only if it increases access to good provision for more children. Confusion arising from a proliferation of definitions would be counter-productive.

Examining definitions is useful in understanding bias and subjectivity. Values are betrayed by the language used. Porter identifies:

> ... a startling array of definitions of what otherwise might have seemed a common-sense concept. This diversity of definitions arises from differences in the ideology and assumptions of their proponents. *1999:32*

Most researchers in the field agree that conceptual difficulties are inevitable (e.g. Freeman, George, and McAlpine, in Porter *op cit*:14) and empirical research excites controversy, contradiction and confusion. For example, inconclusive studies on sleep patterns of the highly able suggest that the able could need either more sleep or less than average. Teachers therefore tend to rely on intuitive identification, such as recognising 'a spark in the eye', 'that switched-on look' or 'a face lighting up', all of which have been offered to me as part of the teacher's battery of identification tactics. Although relevant, these are insubstantial in terms of deciding who should be part of a group receiving targeted provision (Hunsaker, 1994).

In every definition, intelligence is implied as part of the equation. Some theorists present their own view of intelligence, but this can be rather woolly:

> ...intelligence as a construct – that is, an abstract idea that has been invented to explain outward behaviours – whose definition will differ across cultures and which is not so much a characteristic of the individual as a result of experience or learning. *Porter ibid:16, partly citing Khatena, 1992*

This does not give us a clear idea of what is meant by intelligence. A number of notions could replace the word 'intelligence' – try 'anger', 'compassion', 'disgust' or 'humour'. I mention intelligence here to highlight its importance and expand some of this discussion later in this chapter.

With so many definitions and such confusion within definitions, can we manage without one? Theorists have suggested that giftedness is a dynamic concept and, as it is always changing, it cannot be defined without taking account of its development and growth. In this sense, it could be viewed as 'communication and expression of feeling' (Leyden, 1998:3).

Freeman (1998) supports this Vygotskian perspective in her Dynamic Theory of Giftedness (DTG), encouraging children to operate in their Zone of Proximal Development, recognising individual starting points and overcoming difficulties to go on to success.[4] These theories, or 'Dynamic Assessment Procedures' measure changing abilities, in place of a snapshot, one-off IQ score.

In sum,

> Arguments about precise definitions and the identification of
> such children have been active for nearly a century, and will
> doubtless continue. Research shows that the able are not a
> homogeneous group, whether in terms of learning style,
> creativity, speed of development, personality or social be-
> haviour. *Freeman, 1998:1 and 2*

> [Thus] the gifted are clearly a very heterogeneous set of
> persons and it is this multidimensional heterogeneity which
> may preclude a comprehensive theory. The absence of such a
> theory, however, does not prevent us from deepening our in-
> sights and understandings of the phenomena nor intensifying
> efforts to identify talent potential and nurture talented perfor-
> mance. *Monks, Heller and Passow, 2000:841-2*

Definitions of high ability are nebulous and disparate and discussion is difficult without widely agreed terms of reference. So we
do need to find ways of talking about the able. But which words
should we use?

The meaning of words

It is not just philosophically important to be clear about the meanings of words. Teachers affect how children think about their own
strengths and weaknesses through the labels they assign. Labels
can be 'accurate or misleading, negative or positive, a burden or
welcome recognition (Fisher, 1981:49). Many of the terms describing the highly able are insulting rather than flattering. Who
wants to be a boffin, nerd, geek, egg-head, swot or brain box?
Perhaps this is indicative of our culture's view of the more able
person in general. Some of the terms, such as 'precocious', are
innocuous but have been loaded with unwelcome and undesirable
meaning. Dictionaries define precocious as 'being ahead in
development' (Collins) but teachers use it to describe children
thrust forward by pushy parents, performing dinner party turns or
showing off encyclopaedic knowledge. This also holds true for
'prodigy' ('A prodigy is a child who, before the age of 10, performs
at the level of a highly trained adult in some cognitively demanding
domain' (Morelock and Feldman, 2000:227).

Then there are 'the ables'. Researchers use preceding words to create subtle distinctions such as 'more', 'very', 'severely' and 'profoundly', but it is not clear whether these are objective or even useful. More contentious is 'gifted', adopted by UK policy makers and so commonly used 'it would be verging on the deviant to avoid it' (Freeman, 1998:1).[5] The field is generally known as 'gifted education', but the words 'gifted' and 'talented' are understood in a variety of ways. One may refer to a specific ability in one area, and the other to all-round general abilities. Sometimes 'gift' is raw ability, with 'talent' being developed power; sometimes it's the reverse. Teachers and researchers rarely agree on definitive definitions.

- Talent is seen to reflect a remarkable ability which, however, falls short of the superlative level characterised by true giftedness *Braggett, 1997 and Morelock, 1996, in Porter, 1999:31-33*

- Giftedness – innate capacities or advanced development potential, and talent – developed abilities or performances. The term can only be applied to behaviours, not to people *Gagné, 1997*

- The words are synonymous, and can be used interchangeably *Tannenbaum, 1983*

- Giftedness: exceptional competence in one or more domains of ability; talent: exceptional performance in one or more domains of human activity. Genetically determined gifts form the infrastructure for talent development, while personal factors ... environmental constituents ... and systematic learning and training serve as catalysts for the expression of talent *Gagné 1985, 1993 in Schoon, 2000:214*

- Giftedness and talent are terms which have been variously defined over the years and a variety of conceptions have emerged related to these diverse definitions *Monks, Heller and Passow, 2000:842*

- Giftedness is a 'fuzzy concept' *Eysenck and Barrett, 1993 in Porter, op cit*

- The precise definition of giftedness remains a question with no universally accepted answer *Renzulli, 1982*

Language also reveals values held by the society using the words. German and French words for gifted associate the concept with elitism. This 'belief that gifted education is elitist, ... has been a 'limiting factor in developing gifted/talented programs' in Germany, whilst in France no state support is offered for the same reasons (Monks and Mason, 2000:144).[6]

Here I have favoured the use of the term 'highly able' for the majority of able pupils and 'exceptionally able' for the particularly outstanding. When using 'gifted and talented' I am referring to the government strategy, or to specific aspects of literature.

Everyday talk about intelligence

Generally accepted meanings of intelligence also need closer examination when they relate to education. The apparently common sense concept is controversial, complex and confusing, but often used without careful consideration. Although the idea touches the lives of most people, not much turns on its meaning in everyday conversation. Whether or not the use of 'intelligence' is supported by theory or conceptually sound is generally irrelevant. In education, psychology and policy making, however, an examination of underlying assumptions is essential, in the same way as it is with definitions of high ability, as it may determine provision (for example, the 11-plus examination).

Teachers are well placed to observe how their pupils learn. They can present them tasks that enable them to demonstrate their aptitudes and abilities over time, rather than in a one-off test. However, the rise of political correctness and the threat of potential ramifications have made teachers reluctant to use their professional judgement about students' abilities.[7] The notion that intelligence is demonstrated by school results is challenged by the real life stories of those who have defied their apparent lack of ability by demonstrating significant accomplishments. So teachers have become unwilling to assign specific labels of intelligence to children, for fear of missing a not yet discernible special ability.

There is a contradiction here, however. Teachers still display a curious adherence to the notion of IQ, often considering it synonymous with intelligence.

> They continue to believe that it is possible to define a child's level of ability by the use of a test and to give it a numerical score. *Eyre, 1997:3*

Psychology is the field with the largest body of work on the concept of intelligence. Ideas have been so dominant that they have seeped into common usage, but everyday application of the concept has not been subject to rigours of academic argument and discussion. This allows ideas based on inaccuracies to dominate. When new evidence is presented, it can take a long while for public perception to change and meanwhile pseudo-scientific ideas are accepted as fact.

> Intelligence is a topic more written about by psychologists than philosophers. ... Everyone will know about the controversies over the IQ that have preoccupied psychologists for most of the twentieth century. *White, 2002:78*

> Not surprisingly, perhaps, surveys have shown a close correspondence between 'scientific' and 'popular' notions of intelligence *Richardson, 1991:3*

What are the effects of such commonly held conceptions of intelligence? Siblings are often afforded different opportunities by their carers, based upon notions of intelligence: extra chess lessons for the bright girl and French tuition for the boy who might not make it through his exams. The assessment of intelligence levels is usually based on school performance, showing how far-reaching such influences can be. Teachers plan classes and support to provide for individual needs, or decide who should move to a higher or lower set or stream, while many schools still select pupils based on their intelligence as divined through pencil and paper tests. Our successes and failures at school and in life are often 'explained' or confounded by the consensus of our apparent level of intelligence: 'Only the one 'A'? Really? But she's such a bright girl.' In a wider context, doors are opened or closed as result of this contested notion of quality or quantity of intelligence. The gravity of the situation is shown by the increase in employers' use of psychometric tests and scores as part of their recruitment process and possibly also for university entrance.[8] These tests are premised upon the quantifiability of intelligence, aptitude and potential. It is rather a surprising status for such a nebulous notion. It is clear, therefore, that the concept needs critical examination.

So how is the word 'intelligence' used in common parlance? 'Freddie is not at all intelligent'; 'Norah is quite intelligent'; 'Erroll is very intelligent'. Most often it is meant as a capacity, or kind of internal mental strength but it is also frequently understood that this capacity can be employed effectively or ineffectively. Thus we can say: 'Freddie might not be too intelligent but he makes the most of what he's got'; 'Yes, Erroll is a really intelligent boy, but he doesn't apply himself'. This distinguishes between capacity and performance, but still makes use of a central mental power or mental mechanism model.

Intelligence is generally considered a good thing, but only if served up in the right sized portion. Too much is rather threatening and can be isolating and unattractive. Too little is problematic, although this can be compensated for. Mostly, however, people require their friends and life partner to be intelligent. Many a lonely hearts advert mentions this quality, apparently prizing it above physical attractiveness, independent means, love of travel, or a GSOH (good sense of humour) and treating it as the same kind of quality. This would imply a fixed characteristic, like skin colour. It is quite clear, then, that people have an idea of what they mean when they think about 'intelligence' and the personal qualities implied therein. Subtle nuances in language illustrate the concept's complexity and betray accompanying values. The metaphors and imagery are telling. Few people would want to be called 'dull' or 'dim' rather than 'bright' or 'sparky'.

Intelligence is used in a multitude of contexts and scenarios, describing creatures such as highly acclaimed poets to boxers, criminals and dolphins. The poet is a wordsmith *extraordinaire* and the dolphin displays human characteristics of sophisticated communication, amazing memory and expressive playfulness. There is no obvious defining element to these widely differing conceptions. As Richardson observes:

> Just because we have a name for something does not mean that the term has a clear referent; nor does it mean that it corresponds with anything actually existing. *op cit:2*

Intelligence is mostly viewed as an endowment that we all possess to a certain degree, and that this must be fixed and measurable.

This capacity model is a common understanding, explaining the persistence of the importance placed on IQ scores.

Other uses of the term exist. Winch suggests that it is only psychologists who subscribe to the model of intelligence as a processing ability, presenting examples of how the word is commonly used in speech and contrasting this with (Spearman's) notions of a unitary property of the mind. He cites examples of adjectival uses of the term:

> We have no difficulty with such expressions as 'he is an intelligent footballer' or 'she handled that parent in an intelligent manner'. *Winch, 1990:7*

I agree that we infer dispositional characteristics from such uses, linking intelligence to specific activities and behaviour. However, this is more a description of proficiency and the result of experience than intelligence. When people talk of 'an intelligent footballer' the context usually determines what they mean by it and how it relates to the person in question. It could mean that the person 'is intelligent and a footballer', which could still imply the psychological central processing or capacity model. I think this is what people often understand by intelligence. The alternative interpretation would be that the footballer 'plays intelligently', meaning 'skilfully'. Football skills involve concept application and the flexible adaptation of means to ends, as well as physical skills. We generally say that someone is intelligent and possibly use this to explain why they are 'good at' *x* not 'intelligent at' *x*. The confusion arises over the use of 'intelligence' as synonymous with 'intellectual capacity' and sometimes with 'skilful'. Both uses are found in everyday language and nuances of speech or writing often indicate the particular meaning. Just because we are comfortable saying 'She handled that parent in an intelligent manner', does not mean that we do not also have a conception of 'intelligence' as noun, representing the capacity understood as the psychologists' central processing model. In that instance, the intelligence described is general and a property of the mind and in the other it is about performance. To achieve clarity, words such as 'skills', 'talents' and 'abilities' need to be distinguished from one another, and from the term 'intelligence'.

In everyday usage, intelligence is frequently used as an explanation, but trying to explain can end up as a circular argument. 'Chet is a talented trumpeter because he plays the trumpet well. Chet plays the trumpet well because he is a talented trumpeter'.

> Although the level of someone's intelligence is frequently put forward as being a possible reason for that person's success or failure at intellectual tasks, intelligence level is in reality only a descriptive measure, not an explanatory concept. ... invoking someone's high measured intelligence in order to explain a person's success is no more meaningful than putting forward productivity as the explanation of a factory's level of output. *Howe, 1988:349-50*

Howe simplifies the issue here. Intelligence is being used to explain a particular performance in terms of a general capacity. Intelligence cannot wholly explain success or failure, but can be used to explain someone's performance. Howe considers that 'a person's level of tested intelligence provides rather little information about that individual, and considerably less than many writers who use the term in psychological literature appear to believe' (p358). This may be so, but does not mean the concept is useless.

Most people do not need precision in their use of the word 'intelligence', but those who consider its nature in their professional life must be clear about what they mean by it. Psychologists, teachers, philosophers, medical staff, social workers and employers need a coherent working definition, though this can vary across fields, as long as it is suitably grounded. It is intriguing to consider the similarities between the aspects of personality, achievement and attitudes that would be highlighted by a teacher of nursery age children and those of a university graduate lecturer. Even within psychology, there is a range of contested concepts, and no clear overall agreement. Howe emphasises this:

> I think there are strong factual grounds for questioning a number of those assumptions about human ability that many people see as self-evidently true, or 'obviously' correct, or just common sense. ... in connection with young people's capabilities, even those assumptions that almost everyone takes for granted may actually be mistaken. That is a serious matter, because the ways in which we adults think about abilities have

practical consequences that affect the lives and fortunes of numerous children. If the beliefs that guide our decisions and actions are faulty, it is entirely possible that we could be denying children opportunities that would help them to thrive, by cutting them off from valuable learning experiences and effectively slamming doors in their faces. *Howe, 1997:28*

How did these understandings arise?

Research into the nature of intelligence and of high ability have focused on similar key core questions and have hit the same controversies. Understandings of high ability can be grouped as conservative or liberal, concerned with multiple or single abilities, and focused on potential or performance (McAlpine, 1996) and notions of intelligence can be considered in the same way. Debates in both areas swing from one extreme to another, like this range:

single capacity	multiple capacities
performance based	based on potential
originating from nature	originating from nurture
traditional	progressive
selective	inclusive

Despite more than 100 years of study, with numerous developments in neuroscience and psychology, not much has significantly changed:

> We know how to measure something called intelligence, but we do not know what has been measured. We do know that whatever has been measured is predictive of performance in academic settings. And we know that what we have measured is influenced by a person's genes. We do not know what, if anything, should be done with this knowledge. A study of the history of research on intelligence may inform us about how prescient our forebears were. In large measure we know what they knew and we do not know what they did not know and what we find controversial and objectionable in their work is equally so today when similar ideas are advanced by our contemporaries. *Brody, in Sternberg, 2000:30-1 (See also Plomin, 1998 and Challoner, 2000 for a useful summary)*

The first research in the field set the tone. Biometrics was born in the nineteenth century, as scientists attempted to quantify everything in the natural world. It was used famously by Francis Galton, who considered intelligence to be both hereditary and measurable. He studied eminent families and their achievements, together with calculations of the physique, reaction times and sensory perception, to establish a measure of intelligence that he claimed could explain differing abilities. His first publications (1865) were used to 'explain' the dominance and superiority of his race over others. From the outset, this field has been beset by controversy over methods, conclusions and use of data.

One of Galton's detractors was Alfred Binet, who was 'astonished by the considerable place reserved to the sensations and simple processes in Galton's work' (1896, cited in Brody *ibid*:17). Binet (with Henri and later Simon) proposed far more complex tests with elements of digit span, simple arithmetic, writing and sentence completion. These were designed to help diagnose children with learning and behavioural difficulties. Over the years, increasingly sophisticated measures to test reasoning, judgement and understanding of abstract ideas were included, and a comprehensive diagnostic test was developed. Binet's impetus to create this quantitative index of abilities was the need to improve the educational experience of 'retarded and abnormal children'. Binet never converted mental age scores to IQ (this was done by Stern in 1912) as he was – rightly, as it turned out – concerned that his tests would be misused.[7]

Other researchers such as Spearman, Terman and Thurstone continued to argue and publish in the field, leaving an overall sense of anger and disagreement over the conclusions of the research. Only Binet's work seems to focus on helping children.

Since these early pioneers, explaining intelligence has been a major field of study, particularly in psychology and neurology. Measurements have been updated and now cortical arousal, analysis of brain activity in problem solving and hemispheric localisation are all investigated, published by key researchers such as Jensen and Eysenck. A number of theorists have investigated high ability, as a kind of anomaly (e.g. Jausovec, 1997 and 2000). The backlash against IQ theory and accusations of 'pseudoscience' has made some psychometricians defensive (Carroll, 1997:48), but despite continuing study and research, the same central questions about the nature of intelligence have yet to be settled.

The most widely accepted notion of intelligence is a group definition, which first appeared in the *Wall Street Journal* in 1994. Here is the 1997 version which does not entirely avoid ambiguous unexplained language:

> Intelligence is a very general mental capability, that among other things, involves the ability to reason, plan, solve problems, think abstractly, comprehend complex ideas, learn quickly and learn from experience. It is not merely book learning, a narrow academic skill, or test-taking smarts. Rather, it reflects a broader and deeper capability for comprehending our surroundings – 'catching on', 'making sense' of things, or 'figuring out' what to do. *Gottfredson, 1997:13*

The nature of high ability

The notion of high ability is complex and controversial. There are so many different definitions and possible explanations that the concept can seem irrelevant and meaningless. However, some people are more able than others of the same age and background, just as some fall below the average. Some are ahead of their age peers by a considerable margin and their achievements are startling. There are others who cannot communicate their true abilities because of personal or social difficulties, but their potential for expression of high ability can be discerned through occasional revealing performance and/or a compelling constellation of characteristics that make such performance likely, if they are given the opportunity. There is no definitive collection of characteristics or features shared by highly able children and not exhibited in the ordinarily able. There are many different ways in which people can be highly able and these will suggest qualities and learning styles that are as wide ranging as the subject areas in which they are able.

Some people have ability in a specific domain. Others seem to present more general abilities, or abilities that cluster around related areas, suggesting that some sets of skills and knowledge are closely linked, existing perhaps as general pre-requisites for some areas of accomplishment. No one defining characteristic feature of high ability can be discerned. Aptitude is a useful guide, however, as even when different cultural values and fields of expertise are considered, there is evidence of easy mental engagement with difficult ideas and activities. This generally leads to increased practice and commitment, which in turn fosters improved performance. Just applying oneself to a task with gusto is not enough to produce an exemplary performance; aptitude is also needed. Aptitude without application will not produce high achievement, however. High ability is founded on the aptitude to do well in a field. When this is combined with commitment and opportunity, success is likely. If factors conspire to prevent the aptitude developing, underachievement will result.

Conclusion

The words used to describe and explain intelligence and high ability warrant scrutiny. Definitions used by policy makers, researchers and teachers are often unclear. The legacy from psychology has soured the way we think about intelligence because of the morally reprehensible use made of data in the first half of the twentieth century. Separating fact from misinterpretation is necessary is the field of gifted education is to benefit from research rather than being held back by out dated ideas.

References

1   For a review of the shift in focus in worldwide gifted education research, see Heller and Schofield, 2000:123-137. Data about age related research is on p136.

2   'Introduced in September 1999, the strategy operates in 1000 secondary and 400 primary schools to help disadvantaged able children, many of whom are underachieving, to reach their full potential. The strand operates in 70 LEAs and by September 2003, up to 200,000 pupils are likely to benefit. The main elements are:

1.   Identifying the gifted and talented cohort – the 5-10% of pupils identified by each school as eligible for the teaching and learning programme;

2.   Introducing a whole school policy for the gifted and talented cohort;

3.   Introducing a distinct in-school teaching and learning programme for the gifted and talented cohort;

4.   Introducing an extensive programme of out of hours study support opportunities for those pupils, provided through local networks.

Each Excellence in Cities (EiC) area has a Strand Co-ordinator (and a School Co-ordinator for each secondary school) and schools are grouped into clusters. Each cluster has formed a network with a range of external partners such as higher education institutions, libraries, museums and businesses to support the provision of out-of-school-hours activities.' DfES website; August 2003.

3   A termly conference is held in November, March and June/July. Delegates and speakers are all invited and comprise of teachers, policy-makers, pupils, academics, students, activity-providers, parents and other interested parties.

4   A frequently cited example of this is the story of Dame Alice Markova who was pushed into ballet in order to help correct her flat feet (Freeman, 1998: 16, among many others).

5   These terms were chosen against the unanimous advice of the advisory panel made up of teachers, examiners, specialist advisors and academics. Evidence was presented to the committee and is reported in the Hansard House of Commons Review (1998-9) in which the term 'high ability' was recommended to the government. 'Gifted and Talented' was adopted by the head of the strategy to avoid time-consuming debate on terms to describe the able as this was considered a waste of time (personal communication with two separate members of the House of Commons Review and Advisory Group from 1998 to 2001/2).

6   German: *Begabung* or *Hochbegabung* French: *doués or surdoés*. See Monks and Mason for a summary of different cultural perspectives and discussion of how 'meanings are tainted by an emotionalism that seems to engulf the concept of giftedness' (p144).

7   His test is still in use today (4th edition) and remains based on the idea that intelligence resides within the individual and is largely, although not exclusively hereditary (Khatena, 1992). Also see Borland, 1986 and Herrnstein and Murray, 1994.

2

Who are the highly able?

An exceptional child: Miles, age 4, Year 1

Miles' parents could see their younger son's giftedness immediately. He could speak at eight months, read before he was two and his school-based achievement outstripped that of his peers by three to four years. At the age of nine he passed his GCSE maths and he was working with Year 11 pupils when still Year 4 age (although accelerated into Year 6). The only way to interest him was to keep him on the Internet, communicating with international chess masters and NASA scientists and to take him to museums, art galleries and special exhibitions as often as possible.

His parents received bursaries and charity funds to enable him to attend a school with small class sizes that was more likely to meet his needs than the local primary, but this precociously talented boy was extremely demanding. There was no subject in which he did not excel, although as he progressed through school he began to be dismissive of some of the more mundane tasks requested of him. Despite his slowing down in completing activities, all the staff agreed that his abilities were exceptional, and particularly his mature and knowledgeable responses in oral tasks. Miles had friends and was generally well liked, but his ability was off-putting for some of his peers. This is easy to see from the extract below, in which he is being matter-of-fact and honest, but which could equally be read as arrogant.

Do you think you're good at learning?

Miles: I'm a really good learner. I can learn anything, and quickly. Of course, there are lots of things I haven't tried to learn and things I'll never get a go at learning, but the ones I've tried are quite easy, mainly. Lucky for me they're the ones that people think are good. It would be annoying to be really good at learning something like remembering the words to adverts or all the numbers on a page of the phone book, because that's no use because computers will do it for you if you like. I could do that too, by the way. But why would I bother?

Having presented the complexities of defining the high able, I now need to make a practical response. There is insufficient space here to deal with the major issues in detail and so I outline some of the contextual aspects of the field of gifted education (Van Tassel-Baska, 2001), including the origins of ability, global aspects, the value of abilities and their moral dimension. I then consider some of the groups of definitions of high ability and make my stipulative definition.

Contexts: the origins of abilities

It is a struggle to write about high ability without recourse to phrases such as 'natural aptitude', 'genetic endowment' and 'real ability', because we tend to consider ability as an innate characteristic. I remain agnostic about the origins of abilities, as it is irrelevant to the way we deal with children in education.

Teachers may consider certain standards to be unattainable for children who do not have particular 'innate aptitude'. Such lowered expectations can prevent people from achieving their potential, even if this is at a lower standard than their peers. Alternatively, the origin of the aptitude may well be environmental. Would education be improved by trying to inculcate every aptitude in every child by a shift in pedagogy? The impossibility of ensuring appropriate support and provision would render most children failures in terms of achieving their potential of excellence in every subject. Choices would still have to be made about who should focus on what and how resources could be allocated to serve both the individual and society for the best.

It is possible to raise expectations and standards, whether we interpret high ability as innate or as environmentally created. Even were it entirely environmental, the opportunity for developing aptitudes would be affected by the age at which the skills and ideas were first introduced and how they were nurtured. Such early childhood influences would be beyond the control of education.

The role of schools and teachers is to help each pupil, whatever the source of abilities. Pupils with greater aptitudes still need support in order to flourish. All pupils should be helped to see how they fare in a range of fields. What education can do is allow the development and expression of aptitudes, inculcate dispositions and encourage positive propensities. Motivation and opportunity are also vital.

Contexts: global perspectives

In the following chapter, I consider the importance of different global contexts with reference to equality of provision. It is worth mentioning that definitions of high ability vary across cultures. In some cultures the responsibility to make use of gifts to help others is built into the notion of high ability. Others focus on an individualistic, personal interpretation, whereby abilities are used to further careers, increase status and personal wealth.[1] Social and political issues affect how talent is perceived, understood and harnessed. By looking at similarities and differences across cultures, we can learn about alternatives that help improve current practice. Rudnitski observes the existence of multiple perspectives and wonders about policy cohesion:

> What is socially valued varies from culture to culture, so even if it were possible to have homogeneous societies, the definitions of giftedness would have to be fluid to change over time. [...] New models that reflect the needs of a global, information society and economy are needed. *2000:674 and 678*

Disappointingly, the UK Gifted and Talented strategy fails to refer to international research. The global literature may not have all the answers, but we could avoid making mistakes by reviewing ideas already carefully considered in similar societies.

So, social construction obviously affects understanding of high ability, as reflected in the different conceptions.

Contexts: the value of different abilities

It would be (practically) impossible to function if we accepted every skill as equal in importance and so some abilities are considered more valuable than others. A trivial aptitude is nonetheless an aptitude, just of less value or social use than some others.

Traditional hierarchies of academic subjects rate some aptitudes as more important than others. In school, theoretical abilities are generally valued above practical skills, as encapsulated in the contrast of status between vocational and grammar-style education. Such ideas have been challenged in recent years, with multiple intelligence theories changing how curriculum subjects are viewed, and a growing emphasis on valuing all pupils for what they can achieve. The value of an ability is framed in part by the social context and also through the complexity of the task. According to some, if only a few people are capable of a task, it becomes more valuable, although this can only be a reflection of the task when equal opportunity to pursue its accomplishment is allowed. Here I consider intellectual high ability in particular, although not because this is more important than ability in other areas such as music, art, drama and sport.

Contexts: the moral dimension

A definition of high ability does not need a moral dimension to be coherent. However, since education does not take place in a value-less arena, the context of family, schools and society must be taken into account, together with implications for the moral dimension of high ability. Commonly used words 'gift' and 'gifted' remain imbued with religious connotations:

> Exceptional performances have always fascinated mankind, but it was only when the theoretical concepts which resulted from empirical psychological investigation were available, that one could replace the theological and metaphysical explanations which have been hitherto pressed into service. *Ziegler and Heller, 2000:19*

Overtones of 'God-given endowments' flavour the language of 'gift', with its implication of 'goodness', a sense of responsibility and even purpose or vocation.[2] People in general and children in particular can be repeatedly reminded of their 'gift' and told how lucky they are and that they have a duty to make full use of their potential. This can lead to grave disappointment and frustration when 'gift' creates unbearable pressure. A non-religious interpretation of the word 'gift' is that it is a special innate ability. Even without the religious overtones, the ability is imbued with a feeling of responsibility.

Highly able pupils concerned about impending examinations are often told not to worry, because they are lucky enough to be gifted, thus implying that they cruise effortlessly through school-work. This is unfair. Worse still, some pupils' hard earned results are dismissed with an off-hand response: 'We wouldn't expect any less from a gifted pupil like you'. When students make tasks seem easy, teachers can forget how much work they did to ensure a successful outcome. A careful balance is needed between appreciation, encouragement, constructive criticism and praise.

Even within school, pupils with high abilities are expected to be selfless in using skills to represent their *alma mater*. Significant pressure is applied to children whose footballing or singing abilities may help fill the trophy cabinet. In these days of prospectuses and local newspaper features, the all-round able pupil may find themselves on websites, display boards and a regular feature of the newsletter, especially if they are attractive, or fulfil the required ethnic minority quota.

What about gifted people who will not respond to the moral obligations of their gift? At school this can mean general disruption or just withdrawal, which may lead to long-term underachievement and disaffection. Wider problems result from children choosing to isolate themselves from society. Researchers are at pains to explain that, despite popular belief, the emotional state of highly able people is no different from the population in general (Freeman, 1990; Leyden, 1998; Eyre, 1997). However, some people choose to live outside the law or to defy convention in ways that can be harmful or harmless.[3] When asked to name a gifted leader, who had charisma and strength, most would agree about Mahatma Gandhi and Martin Luther King but balk at the inclusion of Adolf Hitler or Joseph Stalin because of their morally reprehensible acts. Complex issues of politics, economics, culture and belief systems are implied in these examples, but the basic issue remains for many people, giftedness must be to do with goodness.

In a fascinating chapter entitled 'Giftedness: The Ultimate Instrument for Good and Evil', Tannenbaum (2000b) explores the relationship between giftedness and morality. He reviews the impact of 'a rogues' gallery of great minds' such as Joseph Mengele and Joseph Stalin and more controversially considers the effect on their legacies of T.S. Eliot's antisemitism and Pablo Picasso's misogyny. He concludes with

> ...a sincere plea to persist with dedication and imagination in making moral education an integral part of enrichment for the gifted in the hope that it will enhance their learning experiences and encourage them to serve society with guidance from its highest ideas. *p463*

Teachers have a role to play in pointing out the consequences of deviant behaviour for pupils not following expected and accepted paths. But ultimately, teachers have to accept pupils' choices. Pupils must be allowed to exercise their autonomy, but teachers may find it hard to let go if they feel pupils are squandering special, rare talents.

Research has shown that able pupils have a well-developed moral sense. This makes a wider than average gap between understanding and action hard to explain and accept (Pagnin and Andreani, 2000). Children may wilfully disregard the wishes and expectations of parents, siblings, friends and society, because they feel somehow let down. The education system is frequently rated by able pupils as a grave disappointment (Freeman, 2001). Years of dull tasks and time spent waiting for peers to catch up take their toll. Children can feel misunderstood and some use their abilities to undermine the system. Others deviate less intentionally. Frustrated and bored in school, they search for stimulation outside the rules and this can result in absence and the formation of bad habits. Able disaffected pupils may fall so far behind with schoolwork that they end up outside the structures that should be able to help them.

In the UK, Personal, Social and Health Education programmes have been bolstered by Citizenship Studies in the National Curriculum, emphasising pupils' contributions to their local, national and global contexts. More may be expected of the able pupils. After her first term of Year 11, Celia started to complain of missing lessons due to her other commitments. A good singer, she was involved in school and community carol services as well as collecting presents for hospital children and organising the soup run rota. She was in the pantomime and running a chess club with the local feeder primary school and had taken over a charity baking marathon when a friend fell ill. Teachers felt she could miss classes as she was ahead of her peers, but she said the pressure was too great. This is not unusual for the able. Guilt is widely documented as a problem (McAdams, cited in Pasupathi and Staudinger *op cit*:263; Freeman, 1998, 2001). Normally obliging, polite and calm, Celia had become frustrated and angry:

> You tell me what I should give up. Apparently homeless people, the elderly, sick children and Mencap are all dependent on me at the moment. What about my GCSEs? What about my social life? You tell me, who should I let down? *From a taped counselling session, Dec 1999*

There is a disparity between moral cognitive understanding and moral behaviour. The highly able child may have an advanced understanding of aspects of a situation, but lack general maturity (Pagnin and Andreani, *op cit*). Very young highly able children who have a sophisticated comprehension of the rules of a game may lack the social skills to play effectively with peers who cannot keep up with their complex rule structures. As a Senco, I was asked to visit Nursery classes to deal with children whose lack of social ability had led to disruptive behaviour. Other Sencos and co-ordinators of the gifted and talented echo this and there is much anecdotal evidence from conferences, network meetings and discussions with school and psychology-based professionals. Such pupils need help in developing their social and emotional maturity.

Group discussion focuses rational justification of values. ... Intellectually gifted children and adolescents are mainly open to this kind of intervention, as they can better recognise the value of a good reasoning context. Nevertheless, social and emotional aspects also have to be considered: developing good basic relationships, identifying with adult role models, being exposed to language, discourses and values giving meaning to life. *ibid*: 481

Issues of high ability should not be considered in a vacuum. The moral dimension is important in terms of identifying the able and planning appropriate provision.

Definitions

The range of definitions and their origins could constitute a book in themselves. Rather than do a disservice to the complexities of these ideas, I do no more here than list the types of influential research in the field and refer readers to texts that tackle these ideas fully.

Key ideas and contentious notions include the following:

- studies of genius and prodigy: are they a race apart? Or can their extraordinary achievements be explained easily?

- is intelligence a single capacity (the notion of 'g') or is it made up of multiple capacities, as suggested in Gardner's theory of multiple intelligences? (Gardner, 1983, 1999)

- what is meant by the term 'potential'? Can potential ever be measured?

- what is the relationship between performance and potential? Should definitions rely on performance or potential?

- can intelligence be measured?

- can intelligence be altered?

All these questions affect the understanding and definitions of high ability and are discussed in detail and with admirable scholarship in the texts noted in the references.

Underachievement

Surprisingly, underachievers are often neglected.[4] Some under-achieving able pupils are considered undeserving of resources because of their negative attitudes and difficult behaviour. Others are written off because of physical disability or sensory impairment.[5]

A performance model of high ability is not an inclusive approach. It is easy to identify a bright child who produces excellent work, is keen to answer questions and take a full and active role in school. Other invisible children may choose to stay out of the limelight, under-performing for some reason.[6] In recent years, underachievement and disaffection, particularly in boys, have been increasingly studied have attracted government research funding.

Deliberately performing badly at school may seem a strange tactic, but many pupils do so for reasons such as boredom and a dislike of school-work, particularly when the only reward for working hard is being given more of the same tasks (See also Whitmore, 1986). Able children, just like their classmates, need stimulation and inter-action in order to flourish. For the busy teacher, 'the temptation was great to leave the more able to work unaided'. Although this was not to be condoned, 'it was at least understandable' (Lee-Corbin and Denicolo, 1998:35). In my own study, I found that children whom teachers expected to perform averagely without any trouble, resorted to a battery of time-wasting techniques. They tended to make an explicit effort to live up (or down) to their teachers' expectations, even making deliberate errors in order to avoid being put into a work group that was given extra tasks. They made clear decisions about which tasks to complete and which to undertake painfully slowly, based on factors such as the follow-up choices available and the teacher's mood. They were adept at duping their overstretched teachers but were certainly not demon-strating their academic potential. Children will deliberately fail tests to move into a lower set if they can be with friends, or escape from a particular teacher (Hallam and Ireson, 2001).

Even when given exciting tasks and teacher attention, some able pupils will not apply themselves because of peer pressure and the school ethos. They are affected by their age and gender and whether their friendship group is in sympathy with the aims of schooling or not.

> If they do work hard they get called a boff. At Thirsk school boff doesn't necessarily equate with intelligence, as much as diligence – and diligence isn't cool.[7] *Williams, 1995 cited in Lee-Corbin and Denicolo, op cit*

> Few children relish being called 'brain' or 'geek' or 'nerd'. Consequently one of the most favourite of strategies is for gifted students to deny their own giftedness, with the most gifted students being most likely to protest their giftedness (Swiatek, 1995). Many minority students who are gifted feel under additional social pressure to conform to student norms. *Gallagher, op cit:683*

When the child's cultural group holds values that do not match those of the school, deliberate non-compliance is assumed to be bad behaviour triggered by the pupil's lack of understanding rather than being a rational decision (Lee-Corbin and Denicolo, *op cit*). Able children who behave in this way may well be overlooked. Such problems are more likely with able children from a lower socio-economic background, an ethnic or religious minority community and amongst children of Travelling people. Highly able children in these groups are unlikely to be receiving provision designed to meet their needs, partly for reasons of funding, partly through lack of understanding. Many of these bright pupils remain unidentified (*ibid*:57-60).

Some children have learning difficulties that can mask exceptional ability. Most common are problems of a dyslexic nature – the child may have handwriting difficulties which are too often dismissed as laziness or petulance. Others just do not do well in tests.[8] Some very able pupils manage to compensate for learning difficulties for much of their school career and may achieve reasonably, so not attract attention. Teachers have become more aware of such problems and children who have trouble spelling are no longer inevitably assumed to be non-academic.[9] Despite improvements in teachers' understanding of learning problems, busy classrooms and constant demands on their time can mean that problems are missed. Most commonly a very able pupil with a minor difficulty will be wrongly perceived as moderately able but producing poor written work. Kellmer-Pringle noted that the majority of 'able misfits' were:

> ...just doing enough that he [sic] will not be bothered by the teacher. As a result he is often rated average or below average but without being considered a real failure. *1970:20*

Some children's underachievement is due to their sensory impairment, physical disability or lack of language skills. As with pupils trying to cope with learning difficulties, the teacher focuses on remediating what they perceive as the main problem and can fail to recognise high ability. In most schools, an able child with handwriting problems will receive extra handwriting exercises, but these tasks are seldom tailored to their intellectual interests and abilities.

The role of parents is significant (Lee-Corbin and Denicolo *op cit*:21-24). Studies have found, unsurprisingly, that parents' marital and relationship problems negatively affect school pupils' performance through changes in lifestyle and emotional stress. When an underachiever's grades start slipping this is often less visible than for those identified as high achievers.

So when we define the highly able, we should include the underachievers among them. Performance-based definitions should only be used in conjunction with other measures.

Incorporating performance and potential: provision-led definitions

Using a non-achievement based model of high ability for allocating provision will yield inclusive results that allow more pupils to benefit from challenging activities and tasks. Pupils can be encouraged to take on activities based on their abilities and interests, so everyone can express some of their skills (Van Tassel-Baska *et al*, 2002). The talents of underachieving able children could emerge in a freer setting of this type. Such a provision-led definition is used in countries such as China, where Children's Palaces expose all pupils to a range of activities in which they are observed by teachers who assess ability through their play performance in relaxed, free settings open to all (Shi and Zha, 2000).

By observing children working and playing, teachers can plan work that starts at the right level for the child, ensuring challenge and encouraging individualised (or at least differentiated) provision.

> Identification and provision have always been seen as closely linked, in that good provision allows ability to be displayed, whilst good identification leads to provision. *Eyre 1997:19*

Generally, though, the phrase 'provision-led definition' is used differently. It is mostly taken to mean that provision can be made for a certain number of pupils, and this defines who can be listed as highly able. Eyre (*op cit*) notes that definitions of the able are often framed in terms of appropriate provision, and says that this is unavoidable. The current government names the top five to ten per cent of pupils, but this is an unsatisfactory definition (see DfES. gov.uk).

The government will pay for x number of activities for y number of children to attend, thus defining the number of gifted children as y. The proportion of the population defined as 'very able' depends, therefore, upon the level of provision in place. If all provision were cancelled there would be no able people. Or if provision were individualised you could similarly dispense with the term 'very able' as all people would be provided for in terms of their personal needs. Noone would require a label.

Such an individual approach is unrealistic. The most likely scenario is that the school system will continue as we know it and cater for the majority of pupils who perform in a largely predictable way, in terms of their abilities to complete tasks deemed appropriate for their age. Pupils performing outside of these norms will require specific provision, as currently described in Special Educational Needs (SEN) legislation. It must be noted that able children are not included in the definitions of SEN except for the few extreme cases of statemented individuals. Children receiving support for SEN normally have some kind of learning difficulty or problem that triggered the provision of help. It is very much up to the discretion of the school, teacher and local education authority as to how such pupils have their needs met. (Porter presents a model of assessment through provision that could be adopted, 1999:104.)

In terms of sound activities and excellent classroom ideas, most source books seem to advocate little more than accepted good pedagogical practice, within a broadly based liberal arts curriculum. There is an emphasis, in books for the able, on breaking down stereotypes of ability and helping teachers to value pupils, whatever their talents, by allowing them to respond in different ways from the usual written requirements. This may be an improvement on the rigidity of the National Curriculum but it does not really answer the needs of able children, who may well be approaching tasks in quite a different way from their peers. More radical provision would probably be appropriate.

Defining what is meant by potential is difficult. Deciding what counts as evidence of potential and providing a way to measure potential is virtually impossible. This is an inappropriate place to discuss such issues, but it would be helpful to make use of philosophical notions to help clarify terminology and concepts (see Scheffler, 1985).

Ultimately, providing opportunities to all pupils may help teachers pick up detailed information about their pupils' abilities, but this would merely be identification rather than a definition or explanation of high ability.

What is meant by 'high ability'?

My characterisation of high ability owes a great deal to definitions and research already mentioned, as well as to personal observations and practice. Sometimes disagreeing and engaging with ideas distant from my own position have influenced me most. As we have seen, the area is nebulous and fraught with difficulty.

My definition is to be read as loose and soft, not strong and rigid. It hinges on some aspects of the traditional views that are worth salvaging from the negative reaction to the single capacity theory that has characterised much theory over the last twenty years, rather than taking one side or the other. I consider the research on the origins of abilities and nature-nurture argument as distracting from the definition rather than being of central importance, because schools need to nurture pupils and provide for their development, regardless of where ability originates.

I focus on *intellectual* high ability and consequently the definition is stipulative. I reject the hierarchy of subjects that holds mathematics, science and language to be of more value than other subject areas, but I omit extended discussion of the skills and abilities involved in practical music, sport and making art. I do so for two reasons, neither of which have anything to do with the value of the subject areas. Firstly, skill development in these subjects behaves very differently from the development of intellectual abilities (Heller *et al*, 2000; Porter, 1999; Eyre, 1997; Freeman, 2001). There are well-researched ways of predicting potential high achievement closely tied to practical fields. Secondly, I am concerned with appropriate provision for developing skills in school and, despite the narrow nature of the National Curriculum (NC), children with special abilities in the practical areas can often pursue their interest through appropriate clubs, and facilities are made available for their development. But the same does not apply to intellectual pursuits, partly because they are tackled in the NC and partly because they have minority interest outside of the classroom. This is not to say that the extra-curricular facilities for all subjects are adequate, just that they are better developed for certain subject areas than others. This makes success more socially acceptable amongst peers; pursuing sport, music and drama is lauded by pupils, whereas pursuing academic study outside of school is ridiculed (Freeman, 2001). For the purposes of this discussion I am adopting a simple dichotomy, dividing subjects loosely into intellectual and non-intellectual.

There is less controversy about aptitudes for music, drama, art and sport than for history and physics. Traits such as such as drive, resilience and perseverance are recognised as necessary for success, whereas the 'possession' of high intelligence is a good enough explanation for doing well in intellectual subjects.[10] Success in all domains (intellectual or non-intellectual) requires a significant investment of time and practice, as well as knowledge and experience. Just as the value of practice is less emphasised in intellectual domains, so knowledge tends to be ignored in the non-intellectual.

The rejection of 'g'-centric notions has allowed for an opening up of definitions of the highly able and a re-examination of how we value non-academic abilities (not just subjects, but qualities such as Gardner's inter- and intra-personal intelligences, 1983). However, the backlash against single-factor intelligence theory has resulted in some elements of the theory being discarded unnecessarily. Just as the concept of intellectual ability brings together a range of subject areas, so certain abilities are implied, suggesting that there may be some value in ideas of a general capacity. Some elements of general ability seem to be untenable, or at least contestable, but others make sense both in theory and in practice. There is a clear precedent for having a range of conceptions of high ability:

> There is no ideal way to measure intelligence and therefore we must avoid the typical practice of believing that if we know a person's IQ score, we also know his or her intelligence. ...we have cited these concerns to highlight the even larger problem of isolating a unitary definition of giftedness. At the very least, we will always have several conceptions (and therefore definitions) of giftedness. *Renzulli and Reis, 2000: 369*

This book focuses on only one area. The highly able child is someone who has significantly greater aptitude for some aspect of intellectual learning than would be considered typical for their age and background. Aptitude for learning is demonstrated through some form of achievement, conventional or unconventional, including notable, isolated incidences that serve as evidence of special ability but are otherwise difficult to categorise.

I deal with five possible objections to this definition, but first I expand the central notion of an aptitude. People can have aptitudes for a wider range of ideas than intellectual subjects, but the focus here is narrow, and so, for my argument, aptitude can be defined as a particular ease in ability progression once the learning process is underway, characterised in intellectual domains as an easy and effective mental engagement with complex ideas in the subject matter.

Not many theorists write about aptitudes, preferring instead the language of gift and talent, but Freeman notes that an aptitude is 'sufficient ability to gain a foothold in the learning process' (1998:7), suggesting an understanding that is not reliant on performance alone. Gagné considers aptitudes within high ability as 'the possession and use of untrained and spontaneously expressed natural abilities to a degree that places an individual among the top 10% of age peers' (Gagné, 2000:67. The percentage differentiation here is impractical and restrictive, but in the context of Gagné's study it was relevant). This inclusive definition considers potential, allowing for beginner learners or people without experience, as well as those who already demonstrate mastery (even those with experience and skills will have more to learn). The definition strongly suggests an on-going process, rather than an achievement-based model, although some expression of the aptitude must be visible, however erratically it is expressed.

There seem to be two broad explanations why an aptitude may not be apparent. One is that the aptitude is dormant, a kind of sleeping giant, waiting to be awakened by a specific trigger such as a new subject area at school or an inspirational teacher. Once engaged, the aptitude can be nurtured, allowing for achievement. In the alternative scenario, an aptitude is hidden, prevented from presenting itself by an unseen barrier or blockage. Once the barrier is lifted, by remediating a learning problem, for example, or access to the dominant language, high achievement is allowed. Both sleeping giants and people with invisible barriers can manifest under-achievement. The first group are helped to emerge through a range of enrichment activities and the second group through sympathetic recognition of problems and support.

Breaking down the nature of high ability further results in long lists of characteristics that tend to render the notion of high ability meaningless.

Some possible criticisms

Any definition of high ability will rightly be the focus for critical evaluation. Here, I consider some obvious issues that could potentially be seen as flaws in my account.

a) Too loose – with a soft definition, the conception is too loose to be valid. The children illustrate the lack of homogeneity amongst the highly able, as well as the 'family resemblance' of related factors. Despite supporting some aspects of generalisable intellectual abilities, I am not presenting a clear-cut IQ-style definition. What I offer is a messier notion, but one that is informed by the research as presented in this chapter and also by practice with children, teachers and with clinical and educational psychologists.

A tighter definition would be too rigid for the heterogeneous pupils in question.

b) Too subjective – by basing definitions on minimal and disparate evidence, there is an over-reliance on teacher interpretation and insufficient objective evidence. Psychologists and educators disagree about what constitutes high ability, but themes do recur. My definition allows for subject-based checklists of characteristics that correlate with success in a field as well as the use of professional teacher judgement based on careful observation of qualities and features that may fall outside usual measures (George, 1992; Koshy and Casey, 1996; Eyre, 1997; Wallace, 2000; Freeman, 1998). The best way to help teachers to increase objectivity is to improve their understanding of highly able children and their needs. Through training, accuracy of identification with supporting evidence will improve, even for students demonstrating only rare flashes of ability. Such pupils are likely to be successful with help, but stand little chance if they are not even identified. In the UK there are on-going attempts to address the lack of professional courses and support for teachers.

> Without exception however, there is a need for training of teachers globally which in turn will prepare them to recognise and meet the needs of children from all cultures who exhibit gifted attributes. *Baldwin, Vialle and Clarke 2000:571*

Building an evidence base prevents teacher bias, reducing subjectivity.

c) Too exclusive – focusing on narrow intellectual ability produces an elitist definition, with pupils already favoured by the National Curriculum content yet again the focus of attention. I have explained reasons for focusing on intellectual ability, but I am not going down the traditional route of 'schoolhouse giftedness'. This is defined by Renzulli and Reis.

> Schoolhouse giftedness might also be called test-taking or lesson-learning giftedness. It is the kind most easily measured

by IQ or other cognitive ability tests, and for this reason it is the kind most often used for selecting students for entrance into special programs. *op cit:*369

The pupils for whom I am advocating do not fit into this narrow frame. Of the examples presented, most of the children would fail to be selected for provision according to these criteria; Billie's handwriting and presentation would let her down, Louis and Nat's attitude to testing is too negative for them to do their best, Charlie's attention span and Stan's idiosyncratic approach to set tasks are likely to affect their attainment. It is probable that André and Doris would be accepted on a programme, but they are the most settled children, arguably least in need of something outside of the curriculum.

The definition is not elitist or exclusive, despite its focus on intel-lectual ability. Children with other skills, talents, abilities and aptitudes are considered as different cases, not as excluded. The definition tackles the awkward aspects of high ability, those falling outside traditional test-taking measures. It also incorporates some aspects of more contemporary multiple measures, allowing per-sonal characteristics to be taken into account.

d) Too simplistic – aptitude is not the sole predictor of success. We are considering children of high intellectual ability, but not suggesting that this recognition will ensure their success. Recognition is likely to be necessary, but not sufficient. Children's motivation, work ethic and the learning and home environments are also significant factors in success, as Galton observes.

> By natural ability, I mean those qualities of intellect and dis-position, which urge and qualify a man to perform acts that lead to reputation. I do not mean capacity without zeal, nor zeal with-out capacity, nor even a combination of both of them, without an adequate power of doing a great deal of very laborious work. *1869:161*

Aptitude must be recognised so it can be fostered. Recognising ability does not on its own, guarantee success.

e) Too vague – there is no cut-off point or distinction between different levels of high ability. I offer no absolute for 'qualifying' as highly able.

The definition is flexible and wide-ranging, designed to be dynamic. A pupil who rarely demonstrates their aptitudes may be allowed to pursue activities that ultimately fail to stimulate repetition of their achievement and their involvement only reconsidered when they have had several failures. Others, apparently new, may suddenly show areas of ability and they will be provided with a chance to explore and extend their work.

Pupils who have exceptional abilities are identified along with those whose aptitudes are more modest, yet still above average. The most extreme cases of high ability are rare, impossible to deny and usually catered for by Special Educational Needs procedures. So I focus on highly able pupils, including underachieving and troubled children whose abilities may be harder to detect.

Conclusion

In this book, I am using a stipulative definition of high ability. Despite focusing on intellectual high ability, my definition is not narrow but inclusive, placing emphasis on children who have not yet demonstrated their aptitudes and potential through regular high achievement. I have shown how our understandings of intelligence and high ability have been coloured by the history of development of programmes of study and research into individual differences.

References

1   'New Zealand Maori peoples value a broad range of qualities in the spiritual, affective, aesthetic, intuitive, creative, leadership and cultural domains in addition to Western culture's intellectual emphasis. The Maori emphasis is holistic and group-oriented... Individuals who excel in any domain will use their special abilities in the interests of others.' (Porter *op cit*:32), and 'Aboriginal peoples value talents in such areas as 'healing, lore, story telling, religion, music, crafts, hunting and tracing culture. Individuals who are talented in these domains are expected to be humble and, although recognised for their talent, are not afforded higher status because of it.' (Harslett, cited in Porter, *ibid*)

2   This is one reason why the House of Commons Review recommended the less contentious term 'high ability' (1998-9). Many cultures historically believed that human talents were an endowment of the gods (Hunsaker, 1995, cited in Moon and Rosselli, 2000:501). Also, 'in ancient Greco-Roman culture special intellectual and artistic abilities were believed to come from the Muses' (*ibid*); wisdom, equated with giftedness, has been considered a divine gift (Pasupathi and Staudinger, 2000:253-67); Ziegler and Heller (2000:5) explore Greek, Chinese and Christian religious themes.

3   Perhaps any deviation from the general accepted codes of behaviour can be deemed harmful within some structures. It might seem heavy-handed to suggest this but in the microcosm of school, this is what often happens, with pupils punished for breaking with convention.

4   They were barely mentioned in the first three years of the government's strategy. See the DfEE/DfES 1997-2000, particularly the Gifted and Talented Unit.

5   A project looking at children of high ability with sensory impairments showed that many people (teachers, researchers and lay people) had not considered such a combination could be valid, unless they had close personal contact with people with disabilities (Winstanley, in Montgomery, ed., 2003).

6   'This is not to say that underachievement causes delinquency: both delinquency and underachievement appear to have a prior cause – namely, non-conformity to social norms, or antisocial attitudes and values.' (Porter, *ibid*:232). My MPhil thesis in 1990 looked at able children in ordinary classrooms, observing their behaviour, in particular taking qualitative information about time spent off-task.

7   This research found a culture in which girls were permitted to achieve and to work hard, but boys were unable to work hard if they wished to maintain a valuable social reputation (Williams, 1995:3). Other studies have found the reverse to operate (e.g. Ayles, 1991 cited in Lee-Corbin and Denicolo, 1998: 20). The point is still relevant, however, peer groups and school ethos are variables in pupil underachievement.

8   'Some able pupils make errors because they cannot conceive that the answer could be so simple. Some refuse to complete the test because it is so routine and dull' Eyre, (1997:19), considering whether or not Standard Attainment Targets (SATs) are valuable in identifying the highly able.

9   Montgomery (1996) vigorously points out that spelling problems do not mean lack of ability.

10 See, for example, Bamberger, 1982; Feldman and Goldsmith, 1986; Howe, 1990a; Radford, 1990; Shutter-Dyson and Gabriel, 1986; Winner and Martino, 2000.

PART TWO
Why should we make provision for highly able children?

3

The case for making provision for highly able children

A child with challenging behaviour: Louis, age 13, Year 8

Louis was most often described as 'cheeky'. He rarely completed homework tasks, skipped some lessons and always had a witty riposte for any comment from teachers about his lack of compliance. As he progressed through school, his humour wore increasingly thin. His obvious ability was undermined by his very low achievement. He frustrated teachers by underperforming and although his peers still found him diverting and amusing, he stayed away more and more, angering his parents and causing problems. Louis' flashes of ability were undeniable, but inconsistent.

Do you think you're good at learning?

Louis: Yeah, but I can't be bothered. I can do lots of this work without learning it, but they don't believe me. I could pass the tests, but they won't let you do them until you've done the practice in class, but I don't need it really. [Accurately mimicking his least favoured teacher] 'Do number one. Do number two. Look I don't care if you can do number three, do the others first!' It's annoying.

Introduction

This is the first of three chapters which present a morally defensible position for provision for the highly able. I maintain that able pupils are entitled to be challenged and stimulated by their statutory schooling, even if this requires provision beyond the basic curriculum. This view differs from the more commonly heard alternatives.

As we have seen, trying to describe the able pupil is extremely complex. It requires taking a non-traditional view of ability to allow for the inclusion of highly able children with special educational needs and those who may not show their abilities in conventional ways (Plucker *et al*, 1996). Once high ability is framed in this way, making an argument to support pupils is less controversial, as teachers want to help children who have easily recognisable individual needs.

When children have special educational needs or some linguistic or social disadvantage, provision is compensatory. This is more comfortable for teachers than directing extra funds to the already privileged. Creating an argument for able children who do not have problems is more difficult. Research (in the USA in particular) continues to demonstrate that 'gifted education' programmes are dominated by children already enjoying social advantage and familial support (Sternberg, 1996). In recent decades, governments and educationists have increasingly focused on minority groups and the underprivileged in general education (although underachieving able pupils have rarely fallen into this category). Consequently, and appropriately, less attention has been directed to the development of able achievers. But there are reasons for providing for able pupils who have no specific needs, as well as the underachievers.

Making this case is difficult because provision for the able implies that teachers will be deciding that some pupils are 'superior' to their peers and that those excluded from special activities are less important. Through schooling, society endeavours to redress unfairness, allowing people to do their best, thus breaking down barriers to success. Where there is no need for compensation for disadvantage or any type of difficulty, provision for the able seems only to serve to create an elite group. Whilst other pupils are fighting for scarce resources, provision for the able is seen as at best an unnecessary luxury and at worst a misguided tactic that increases social division and elitism.

These commonly held views need to be challenged. It is important for policy makers, teachers and researchers to be able to articulate their reasons for supporting provision for the able. This section of the book clarifies the terms needed for such articulation and lays out the common arguments for support or refutation. I also present my own notion concerning the quality of cognitive challenge in school – what I call *equality of challenge*.

Political and policy issues

The overriding matter both in literature and in practice is the un-resolved tension between the contradictory dual educational aims of excellence and equity. Although this book is written from a UK-based perspective, many of the issues raised have currency for a broader context. As these matters have to be addressed by all countries, it is both relevant and illuminating to examine the different responses and discern useful general principles or frameworks.

The global context

Despite wide differences between educational systems and cultures, there is a consensus that some pupils seem more able learners than their peers, or seem to have greater potential for achieving in school-based activities. Most countries consider this can contribute to their development and growth, if the children are supported to ensure their potential is translated into achievement. So efforts are made to make appropriate provision while retaining a sense of fairness, particularly in the distribution of education resources and allocation of limited funds. There is no country for which funding is unproblematic. All the issues of identification and provision mentioned so far are magnified when the problem is expanded into a global arena.[1]

Contrasting cultural perspectives of 'giftedness' and policy-making for the able from a range of countries brings to light complexities of justice and fairness that are rarely made explicit in the literature and research. Practices and policies vary, as do the underpinning values. There are competing understandings of the origins and nature of giftedness and of appropriate ways to provide for these pupils.

> ... modern cultures tend to believe that unusual abilities are the result of heredity, environment, individual effort, or some com-

bination of these. Which of the three receives the greatest emphasis in a particular culture can have a dramatic impact on gifted education. *Moon and Rosselli, 2000:501*

This is not the place to examine the various ideas in detail. All I can do here is select some contrasting approaches as an illustration.

In the US and Canada, a prevailing cultural belief is that individual differences in abilities are largely the result of natural endowments. *ibid*

In Canada provision is 'inconsistent, unsystematic and based on practitioner enthusiasm', organised by individual states or local education services (Leroux, 2000:695-6). In the US the equity-excellence pendulum has driven research and provision with a recent focus on finding hidden talent within disadvantaged communities which are viewed as a 'major untapped resource'. The current jumble of provision has some admirable aspects and the US leads the world in research in this field, but the lack of cohesion results in a *laissez-faire* approach (Gallagher, 2000:691). Australia and New Zealand are interesting cases where egalitarian concerns have for some years overridden the needs of the able. After reviewing the poor performance of minority groups, schools tried to redress the balance, particularly from the 1950s to the 1980s.

In its starkest form, the issue was seen in terms of alternatives: education could concentrate on those with special needs (the disadvantaged) or those with special abilities. ... the New Zealand Education Act of 1989 decreed that 'equity objectives shall underpin all activities within the school'. There were moves to downplay the concept of giftedness as such and use different terminology ... highly able, or children with special abilities. *ibid:*780-1

In most developed countries, gifted education is tainted with the hangover of its links with elitism and exclusivity. Modern approaches have equality at their core, as part of the social efficiency argument encouraging all members of society to reach their potential in a range of activities, but public justification for policy is typically rather vague. Various players in government may have a range of reasons for supporting particular policies, but rarely is there coherent public explanation of the aims in question. This is the case even in the in countries with more mature policies. In the US, 'poor and minority students are disproportionately excluded from programs for the gifted' (Kornhaber, 1999). This underscores the difficulty in realising aims, due to issues of wealth distribution. The same problems arise in the UK, where parents who can afford to may move home to take advantage of maintained sector education that best suits their needs. It is also apparent in the explosion of demand for private tutors in areas where 'superior' schooling (defined through measured academic success as reported in league tables) is accessible by passing examinations. In Australia and New Zealand, some states have found their drive for equity incompatible with the success of programmes for the disadvantaged able pupil. Teachers report that they are unable to continue programmes as inequality is being created by allowing the more able to succeed (eg Benbow and Stanley, 1997).

This contradiction is evident in other ways. Some abilities are regarded as fair opportunities for investment, while others are viewed as elite. Gross observes that extra funding for sporting prowess is often considered more acceptable than extra funding for academic areas:

> Both nations (USA and Australia) abhor racial, social, and religious bias. ... yet we do hold a pervasive, insidious bias when it comes to talent development. All gifts are equal, we seem to say, but some gifts are more equal than others. ... Our bias becomes apparent, however, when the children's precocity is sited in the cognitive domain. *Gross, 1999:3*

Myriad articles lament the refusal of leaders and administrators to differentiate exceptional students in the name of equality (for example Lloyd, 1996) and such concerns are seen in cultures as far apart as the Philippines and Korea.

> Democratic societies, whether long established or newly forming, often have reservations about special programmes that meet the needs of only a few – particularly when those programmes expand the gifts of the already talented individuals. However, in the future, as educational strategies and programmes are refined the issue will not be equity versus excellence, but equal opportunities for all students to achieve excellence in their special talents. *Wollam, 1992:67*

In most Asian countries, individual differences are accounted for through effort and 'teacher skill and pupil diligence' are emphasised. In the Philippines, Taiwan and Singapore, some family values forbid differential treatment of siblings which is regarded as unfair. Consequently, highly able children are often denied extra-curricular activities unless their siblings are also involved, even if one child has no particular aptitude or desire for something that is wished for and easily accomplished by the other child. Some countries develop programmes that aim to foster economic development and maximise the nation's human resources. Underlying principles suggest the populace is governed 'on the basis of employing the talented' and a 'societal tendency to value intellectuals and the wise' (Wu, Cho and Munandar, 2000:775).

'Bitter experiences with social elitism' (*ibid*) have led to a strongly egalitarian policy in Japan, where 'gifted education has become almost a taboo subject within Japanese society' (*ibid*:768). There have been some recent moves to cater for older students, but nothing is available for younger pupils.

> This attitude is rooted in a belief that ability is not inherent, but rather the result of practice and hard work, even at the youngest age. [...]Japanese people believe that the individual differences, even at the fetus stage are influenced by the environment and one's efforts rather than by innate, stable and fixed characteristics. Therefore, they believe that the government should not enhance individual differences by intentionally providing special programs for those who are already doing well. p769

This has resulted in an egalitarian provision pattern similar to the Nordic model typical of Sweden, Norway and Denmark, and to a lesser extent, Finland. Ironically, similarities in provision have wholly different roots. Japan is characterised by the 'propensity for embracing and awarding individual excellence' whereas the Scandinavian ideal is of inter-dependence and 'reluctance to reward or promote policies or actions that would cause some individuals to excel more than others' (Persson *et al*, 2000:718).

Nordic provision is exceptionally egalitarian and it is considered improper to exhibit pride of self. Schooling and society reinforce the sense that no one is 'special'.[2]

Swedes are ambivalent about their 'stars' [...] whether in sports, show business, or culture. Successes may be admired, but their exclusiveness and out-of-the-ordinary achievements often give rise to envy and therefore to malicious pleasure when the stars 'fall'. The high value awarded to sameness makes all personal success problematic. *Daun, 1994, cited in ibid:719*

During the Communist period some Eastern European countries denied the existence of genetic variation, and this acted as a barrier to the development of gifted education programmes (for example in Poland). Similar issues arose in Russia and the search for the talented consists of competitions now harnessed to help build profiles for entry into higher education rather than coercion into an identified field of potential excellence (Grigorenko, 2000:739) for the 'enhancement of national honour' (Moon and Rosselli, 2000: 502). In China, psychologists have used the term 'supernormal' to describe the able (since 1978). It conflates two key concepts in gifted education in China: the statistical meaning of being 'relatively superior to most normal children' and the role of God-given talent; 'gifted' in Chinese is *tian cai* which literally translates as 'God's bestowal upon man' (Shi and Zha, 2000:758).

In developing countries, policies have not been cultivated because of other pressing needs, but models now being adopted generally follow the US, Australia or New Zealand. They reject European ideas, as these tend to be rooted in a performance-based understanding of high ability and also very closely linked to a traditional formal schooling system with a long history of perpetuating class divisions. Historical inequity, colonial rules, political struggles, civil unrest and lack of funding have dominated educational development in Africa and Latin America over the last century and the notion of singling out a small group for special treatment unfortunately echoes elitist practices in the past (Taylor and Kokot, 2000:803). There are also cultural understandings of the individual, family and society that affect the development of differentiated education (also in Maori culture, where social and leadership skills are more important than academic achievement). In Africa, the concept of *ujamaa* meaning family, or togetherness represents:

> ... a call for communal co-responsibility towards the upliftment of those in society who, in some or other respect, have remained behind. *ibid:801*

Misconceptions about the able persist in Central and South America, apart from Cuba, where differentiated curricula have been in place since 1991. For the most part, however:

> ...a strong prejudice is firmly rooted in popular and teachers' thinking that any differentiated practice with the gifted threaten equity and democratic principles of education. *Soriano de Alencar et al, 2000:823*

It is commonly considered that able pupils are not in need of specific instruction and that high ability will be clearly evident in every sphere. High ability is equated with high accomplishment and it is also commonly thought that social and emotional troubles are inevitable (*ibid:*823-4).

In every country, finding the optimum way of pursuing fairness is a controversial matter. These examples demonstrate that the issue cannot be overstated and that cultural factors affect ideas of high ability. In sum, and rather baldly dichotomised:

> On the one side, it seems, stand critics who equal talent-selection to creating a socially privileged societal stratum potentially beyond democratic principles. On the other side, stand proponents arguing the democratic rights of children to develop to their full potential. *Persson et al, 2000:703*

The UK and other European countries

In the UK, policy is still in its infancy and current discussion appears dominated by political correctness. The normative percentage-based definition of high ability seems inadequate and gifted education is inseparable from issues of selective schooling and exclusivity.

> Recognising and nurturing high ability has, in a sense, been an integral part of English society for a long time. Interest in high ability, however, has been largely class-bound, and has become a part of the sometimes conflicting interests of the higher and lower strata of English society. *ibid:723*

High ability is not recognised in special needs legislation and the most vociferous campaigners for education for gifted education have been parents' groups. Like other European states (e.g. France and Germany), there is separate school provision for different pupils and geography makes all the difference to the kind of education a pupil is likely to receive. In the UK, there are wholly different systems (comprehensive, selective, independent, public), with resulting inflexibility making it complicated to pass between schools and systems in order to take advantage of the most appropriate provision (Rudnitski, 2000:728). Despite the range of provision, it is still a battle to create provision specifically for the able.

> Due to the dominance of political egalitarian conviction, as in the Scandinavian countries and former Communist Europe, resistance to focus on gifted education as a separate issue in the English school system – irrespective of the existence of traditional elite schools – has been formidable. *ibid:723*

Overwhelming issues – elitism, meritocracy and equality

Concern with elitism, meritocracy and equality pervade discussions of high ability provision all around the world. It is important to be clear what is meant by these terms in order to engage effectively with the debates.

Elitism

In the UK, the government admits confusion over the issue, with New Labour blaming the 'old left' for the muddle:

> We have always wanted to make opportunity open to all, to allow people to progress and improve themselves by merit and hard-work, and to tear down the barriers that prevented the disadvantaged from making a better life for themselves. But we made a mistake. In our determination to open up opportunity to the whole of society, we confused elitism with excellence.[...] We were embarrassed to celebrate excellence, for fear we would be taken for celebrating the elite. ... we created our own set of illusionary taboos. It is time to break them. *Morris, May 2002* [3]

People are naturally averse to elitism where it is synonymous with unfairness. Is this always the case, however? Consider these definitions of elitism:

— some students will do consistently better [...] than other students. They will form an elite with regard to this subject matter.

— a sense in which only a very narrow range of abilities are considered to be educationally worthy and are therefore specially catered for in our education system. *Winch and Gingell, 1999:76*

The first definition is about achieving highly and therefore becoming specialists, whereas the second description makes value judgements. This echoes negative and out-dated aspects of Galtonian and IQ theory (discussed in Part One) which seeks to 'rank human intellectual attributes in an unreasonable manner' (*ibid*:77). In defining elitism, Collins' Dictionary notes:

1. The belief that certain persons or members of certain classes or groups deserve favoured treatment by virtue of their perceived superiority, as in intellect, social status, or financial resources.

    a. The sense of entitlement enjoyed by such a group or class.

    b. Control, rule, or domination by such a group or class.

2. (adj) Selected as the best; 'an elect circle of artists'; 'elite colleges' (n) group or class of persons enjoying superior intellectual or social or economic status.

In everyday usage, elitism is loaded with baggage; people mostly imply the first meaning noted above when they use the word. 'Favoured treatment' should not result from any of the characteristics described and people will rightly reject a system that allows this to happen. The second definition is a jumble. The adjective refers to people who actually are the best at something, whilst the noun is used for status that need not have been earned. The example of 'artists' is perhaps a difficult choice, as it represents a field that is not made up of a clear and objective set of skills but is notoriously victim to fads and fashions. The ability of the artist as draughtsperson can be measured, although the extent of their influence on future generations cannot be instantly assessed. 'Elect' implies chosen and it would depend on the selection criteria as to whether that would form an acceptable or unacceptable group.

Rigorous training and examination are no less than we would expect for aspirant members of the Parachute Regiment or SAS. Most people want our best soldiers in the field, our greatest footballers in the World Cup and most accomplished musicians in our international orchestras. This kind of elite is acceptable.

Other forms of elitism are more confusing. A divine notion of elitism is difficult to refute, as it would entail proof, or not, of a divine being or beings. The selection of the Dalai Lama and the Pope rely on such guidance, and royal families are determined by an alleged divine right. An historic tradition has built up over centuries, ingraining these ideas. Birthright elitism concerns parents giving advantage to their children, and is acceptable to many people. In this case, even when the political ideal of equality is supported, the conflict with other values is too strong to abandon (Swift, 2001). Parents are passing on the benefits of hard-earned wealth, whilst simultaneously contributing to wider society through their taxes. It is an all-things-considered benefit for their children, although it is likely to bring with it some educational advantage. Being able to pass on wealth will probably reflect a life in which aspects of educational advantage can be bought through having time to support children and the pursuit of extra-curricular activities. Swift notes that '...many people say they want 'equality of opportunity' when what they really want ... is actually just less inequality of opportunity' (*ibid*:101).

Social elites are also complex. Families can acquire wealth but still be excluded from the goods to which they aspire. Entire comedy shows are built on the 'joke' of the unsuitable rich social climber, suffering because they are trapped in a lower social stratum than they believe they deserve. We laugh collectively at their delusion, knowing they will never be admitted to the elite club they hanker after.

Forms of exclusion often considered synonymous with elitism concern class, race and gender issues interlaced with the idea of elitism as superior ability. Historically, women, ethnic minorities, homosexuals, people of certain religions, those with disabilities and with lower socio-economic status have been variously excluded from a variety of activities and institutions. The excluding institutions have been dubbed elitist. Disallowing people on an irrelevant basis is abhorrent and intolerable. But this is entirely different from disallowing someone through their lack of actual ability to benefit from a specific activity or membership, for example joining an advanced choir when they cannot read music, or applying for the Magic Circle even though they cannot perform tricks or illusions. This confusion is demonstrated in a recent article considering the nature of the Royal Society and its funding:

> The Royal Society, by its very nature, is an elitist organisation. What else can a national academy of science be? Its whole *raison d'être* is to represent the best of science in this country. ... The word elitist means different things to different people ... elitism has (also) become an all-purpose boo word for condemning any kind of exclusivity, justifiable or not. One doesn't want to be elitist in the sense of saying 'we're only going to have white men' or 'we're only going to have people who went to Oxford', ... the society has an historic problem. *Watts, 2002:18*

In education, sensitivity has grown towards elitism, as the government fights against old-school exclusivity, favouring a meritocratic system in which the able are allowed to achieve highly, without barriers to their accomplishments. The expansion of university places has drawn the criticism that they are 'dumbing down' education.[4] The Prime Minister is determined to make changes, despite some attacks on the apparent rise of the 'parentocracy' (Hellawell, 2002).

> There are some traditionalists who believe that more means worse – that only a minority have the brains to go on to university ... It is a cosy elitism that has bedevilled and weakened our education system for more than a century. *Blair, quoted by Goddard, 2002:3*

Recent initiatives have spawned a new type of complaint. The Faculty of History at Bristol University rejected students with top grades from independent schools in favour of students from state schools who constitute the next level down in terms of achievement.[5] They thought that the state school students would have worked much harder to achieve their grades and would therefore make more committed students. The university considers this a fair and meritocratic process, but some independent schools have complained that this tactic is elitist and Bristol University has been boycotted by some head teachers and careers staff.[6] (It feels ironic to be advocating for the able privileged as a group suffering from discrimination.)

Confusion and emotion surround the concept of elitism. Perhaps it is better avoided. Would it be clearer to distribute resources on the basis of merit?

Meritocracy

Meritocracy is a political system and elitism is not, but they are often falsely dichotomised. Meritocracy can be defined as the principle that:

> ...each person's chance to acquire positions of advantage and the rewards that go with them will depend entirely on his or her talent and effort. In such a society inequalities in different people's life chances will remain, but social institutions will be designed to ensure that favoured positions are assigned on the basis of individual merit (talent times effort) and not allocated randomly, or by ascriptive characteristics such as race or gender, or by the machinations of the already powerful. *Miller, cited in Brighouse 2002:177*

Miller's notion of 'talent times effort' relies on the concept of desert, which is contentious among political philosophers. John Rawls, for example, considers that people cannot be held accountable for their degree of talent and that '... luck plays too great a role in determining how much people can sell their productive activity for' (Swift, *op cit*:40). In the same vein, Harry Brighouse argues against this notion as a suitable principle on which to base the distribution of educational resources. He considers the notion of desert inappropriate, stating that:

> ...natural ability, like social class background is something we cannot reasonably be held responsible for, ... [this] suggests a strongly compensatory principle, that significantly more educational resources should be spent on the less able than the more able. *Brighouse, 2002:40, point 5*

Interestingly, Swift observes that popular opinion endorses the concept of desert whereby people are entitled to earn different amounts even when this is for reasons beyond their control. This clashes with the Rawlsian view and is also disputed by Robert Nozick, who is sympathetic to difference and to some aspects of public opinion as noted here, but not to distribution by desert.

> ...they agree with one another that achieving social justice is not about making sure that people get the value of their productive activity on the grounds that they deserve it (Rawls because of the 'moral arbitariness' objection, Nozick because distributing according to desert is a patterned principle). *Swift, op cit:40*

Swift contrasts three different views of desert: 'conventional'; 'extreme'; and 'mixed'. The 'conventional' view is that noted in the previous paragraph, allowing for inequality in earnings and supported by popular understanding. The 'extreme' view disallows reward for effort as well as talent because it is considered that how hard someone works is out of their control. It is irrelevant whether a strong work ethic is in-born or instilled at an early age, but it should not be an incentive for higher pay. The 'mixed' view allows for rewarding aspects that people can control and choices they have made. Rawls rejects the mixed view because it is impossible to discern which aspects of performance can be derived from one's own efforts.

Teachers tend to hold the mixed view. This can result in children being prevented from participating in enrichment programmes perceived as fun rewards. Children are expected to demonstrate both parts of the merit equation and are disqualified if they are considered lazy. (I am not sure about the concept of laziness in relation to young children in particular; it seems likely that there are other reasons for the behaviour.) Often, children fail to engage with tasks for extenuating reasons not to do with laziness but with emotional or learning problems. Westerners see the work ethic as within the individual's control and believe that any talent should be properly utilised. This contrasts with Asian and Pacific Rim cultures that view talent exclusively as the reward of effort and distribute university places and other educational privileges on the basis of a concept of talent as success earned through endeavour.

Using desert as a basis for provision for the able seems at first sight reasonable; reward for hard work, not as unfair advantage. However, if hard work is as much a result of background influence as other aspects of talent, pupils who are able but have not been encouraged are likely to be excluded from such schemes. High achievers are favoured again and some pupils with potential to benefit from unusual activities can be passed over in favour of those who are less able but more conforming. I have heard talk of the 'able worthies' and the 'able unworthies' in staff meetings for allocating provision, with Louis and Nat topping the list of the 'lazy'.

Some children work hard, while others can achieve the same results with less effort because they have abundant talent. If merit is a basis for reward, there must be a way of ensuring that every child has a fair chance to demonstrate both effort and ability. Underachievers fail to apply themselves for a range of reasons, or give a false impression of exertion which makes it difficult to assess ability accurately or to know how much effort they are expending. Consequently it is unclear what they merit. Astute underachievers can convince teachers and parents that they do not need the extra work bound to follow from a true assessment of their ability (Louis became an expert in this regard). Others do not exert effort because they see little purpose in a set task, and some are so lacking in confidence that they cannot engage with the task at all. It seems that merit is a problematic basis for distributing resources. A different way of considering merit and Miller's concept of meritocracy would be from the perspective of enhancing efficiency rather than desert, as discussed. This is considered in the next chapter.

If desert is to be used as a measure for distributing resources, it is vital to be clear about what is actually meant by desert. Can it be ensured that all children's talent and effort can be accurately measured in order to decide exactly who deserves what?

Equality

Ensuring equality for all children is often espoused by teachers, researchers and policy makers, but it is not clear that they share an understanding of what this equality could mean. Equality of outcome, opportunity and resources have different meanings and implications, but are often viewed as synonymous with fairness, which is a laudable aim. Winch notes that the principle of equality of treatment

> ...requires that goods and outcomes be allocated equally to all, regardless of factors of entitlement, need or desert. *1996:115*

Few teachers would ignore entitlement, need and desert when deciding how to allocate resources.

> What matters is not that people have equal shares of good things. Nor is it even that people have equal opportunity (or access to) good things. What matters, if we think about it, is that everybody has enough, or that those who have least have as much as possible, or that people who most need things take priority. *Swift, 2001:92* [8]

White rejects both egalitarianism and equality, emphasising that this does not imply that he accepts right-wing views of education. Meeting needs should be separated from valuing equality, and equal access to leading a flourishing life need not mean equal distribution of goods (1994:174). White cites Raz, emphasising that the real concern is not for equality, but for the suffering or need of the individual in question. We may redistribute goods, but this will be for reasons of relieving hardship, not for creating equality (p175). According to White, this supports the notion that '...one has good reason to attend more to the needs of those more lacking' (p180), which would seem to rule out most, but not all, able pupils. Were it feasible to separate ability and achievement, pupils with a large performance-potential gap could be viewed as lacking.

Rawls' principles underlie my ideas about the fair equality of opportunity principle, which appears on the surface to be a meritocratic principle, insulating educational opportunities from class difference. It allows more resources for the able, until the difference principle is considered. This principle operates as long as social class has no influence over social equality, but given the state of our unequal society and the small number of highly able people, the greatest benefit to the least advantaged is unlikely to be served by giving more to the able.

It seems that equality arguments will be of little use in supporting resources for the able. But what exactly is meant by equality? The literature tends to focus on three areas of equality: resources, opportunity and outcome.

Resources: Brighouse argues that it would be fair to spend the same amount of money on each student's education (1995:418). He rejects the way John Wilson problematises this notion. However, it is unclear how equality of resources could be made to work and even whether or not it would be desirable. Some training and learning is just more costly and it would be unnecessary and prohibitive to fund-match for all potential students. In their papers, Wilson is referring to university education and Brighouse to schooling, but neither is completely clear about boundaries for provision, although this would be important in trying to create a funding formula or policy. In a footnote (p149), Brighouse acknowledges this difficulty, recognising that the difference with Higher Education is that it is applicable to adults, who should be freer to make their own choices. While this is relevant, it worth noting that access to Higher Education is often determined during schooling, where some groups of less privileged people are ruled out and others virtually guaranteed participation.

Brighouse rightly criticises Wilson's woolly notion of resources being awarded to those who can 'profit from them most'. What is meant by 'profit most'? If interpreted as gaining the highest grades, it could apparently be advantageous to able achievers. If the profit is calculated as value added, disadvantaged or weak students should be the key beneficiaries, but if profit is measured by enjoyment, it would be children with an enthusiastic disposition. What would happen if the investment failed to reap benefits? Resources should be distributed according to need, favouring underachieving able children over high achievers in order to increase the likelihood of their success, even if resources are ultimately distributed unequally.

Opportunity: Swift identifies three understandings of equality of opportunity: 'minimal', 'conventional', and 'radical' (*op cit*:91). According to the minimal view people's gender, religion, race, etc, must not prevent them from opportunities in, for example, education and employment. The conventional view goes further. Not only should people's competences be considered above their race, etc, but they should have had an equal chance to acquire the competences in the first place. This echoes the meritocratic principle of rewards for talent times effort, with the added dimension of aiming to assure a level playing field. Many people like this idea but balk at some of the measures required to ensure its realisation, for instance restricting or demanding certain practices in the home, such as supporting children with homework. Without equalising parental support, 'conventional' equality of opportunity cannot be assured.

The third conception of equality of opportunity is labelled 'radical' and 'requires that untalented children – whether rich or poor – should have the same opportunities as talented children' (p102), which again would oblige the state to revise some deep-seated structures and values, such as the meritocratic aims it seems to hold. It is difficult to say exactly what is meant by equality of opportunity, as it is not even clear what opportunities are in question.

Outcome: Equality of outcome is also complex and open to a range of interpretations.

> Equality of outcome is a principle of equality that asserts that the endpoint of a process ought to be the same for everyone who goes through it. *Winch, 1996:115*

It is difficult to define the 'endpoint' and the 'process' in education and so this view can be interpreted along a spectrum from a weak to a strong conception. A weak notion would require something like the National Curriculum, which is a fairly rich minimum of educational experience, covering a reasonable range of subjects and assuming that children should emerge from school with roughly the same set of life skills. Even with this conception, highly able children without problems are likely to complete their requirements earlier than their peers, but are still expected to stay in school. With equality of outcome they would be unable to undertake additional work so would be wasting time. However, if the standards were raised to meet their abilities, many other children would be unable ever to reach the same high levels and the cost of trying to do so would probably be prohibitive.

A stronger interpretation would require specificity about the school experience or process, implying less diversity in schooling. To allow everyone to achieve the same endpoint, teaching would have to be in far smaller groups, or minimum levels would need to be set at a fairly low level. We can see the effect of these ideas by looking at the issues raised by various Swedish and Australian programmes of education (Feather, 1989).

Conclusion

It is important to consider the needs of the highly able, but many of the factors that impact on these pupils are mired in controversial and emotive areas. Account must be taken of the needs of pupils in discussion that is free from unnecessary historical hostility to provision for the able.

We move on to examine the arguments for and against providing for the able.

References

1   Rudnitski in Heller *et al* (*ibid*) points out that if governments worldwide prioritised education in any way that could be considered close to military budgeting, there would be sufficient funding for a huge range of programmes and no need to take from one group to give to another.

2   The expression 'the Law of Jante' encapsulates this and was first used by the Danish novelist Aksel Sandmose in 1933 (cited by Persson *et al*, 2000: 718).

3   Estelle Morris, (Secretary of State for Education), speaking at the Institute for Mechanical Engineering on 16 May 2002. The speech can be accessed at www.dfes.gov.uk/speeches. The speech is a little confusing concerning under-performing pupils. Surely they are not suggesting that effort should no longer be put into helping these people?

4   There have been recent news reports suggesting that university entrance could be decided by a lottery (4 September 2003, BBC Radio 4), to avoid subjectivity in admissions procedures. There have been calls to introduce North American style Scholastic Aptitude Tests (12 October 2003, BBC Radio 4) and the serious political fall-out from the 'top-up fees debate' (in the public arena from November 2003 and still raging in January 2004).

5   I call these children 'the marzipan layer' during Inset sessions and teachers have found useful. The pupils are often forgotten, their needs superseded by the more obviously able pupils, or those with clearly observed difficulties.

6   M. Hodge (Minister for Higher Education) at the Social Market Foundation think-tank, London. 'The minister praised a scheme run by the history department at Bristol University where the average A-level score for the school was taken into account before a place was awarded. If a state school pupil had significantly outperformed their predecessors, they were awarded places even if they had 'far lower A-level qualifications' than Bristol had accepted in the past. The government was determined that more working-class youngsters should get the benefit of going into higher education. The target ... was not a matter of political correctness, but vital for the future of the economy. Tim Cole (Bristol University) denied suggestions that pupils from private schools were losing out under its selection scheme' (April 12 2002).

7   Patterned principles 'prescribe a particular state that must be realised (such that inequalities are benefiting the worst off) or require distributions in accordance with a particular pattern' (Swift, 2001:34).

8   Differentiating again between social and school policy, while most teachers would agree with Swift about what matters, they would also want to take into account Kymlicka's notion of an 'egalitarian plateau'; the principle that 'members of a political community should be treated as equals, that the state should treat its citizens with equal concern and respect' (cited in Swift, 2001:93).

4

The usual suspects:
common arguments for and against
providing for the highly able

An unusual child: Stan, age 4, Reception

Stan would infuriate his mother and teachers by speaking in rhyme, or saying the last word of each sentence backwards. He would play with words all the time and his peers would find it hard to understand him, describing him as 'odd' or 'funny'. He was particularly fascinated by the etymology of words and would tell people whether words had Greek, Latin or Anglo-Saxon roots. He was also a mine of information, constantly spouting obscure general knowledge facts and making word play jokes that only adults would understand. He found it hard to make friends of his own age.

Do you think you're good at learning?

Stan: Learning is learning and earning is earning. I have learnt some good things over the years, but there's a lot I haven't put to memorisation yet. Can I go back to class now?

This chapter is presented as a series of arguments commonly used in debate about resourcing the able. The first four maintain that providing for the able is a bad use of scarce educational resources and the following five make the case that the able merit provision. I show where these arguments are problematic.

Arguments against providing for the highly able

Argument 1 (against): provision for the highly able is elitist

It is suggested that providing for the able prevents other pupils from benefiting from provision, resulting in elitist practices. There is no reason, however, why providing for the able should be elitist in the negative sense of the word, if suitable criteria are applied. There is little point designing activities of no value to potential participants. Restricting them to people who have the requisite skills, experience or interest is acceptable. Restrictions that are made for no reason are unacceptable.

There could be a case for reclaiming the word elitism and focusing on its benefits. We have seen, though, that the notion of elitism is contested and loaded with baggage, so the label is perhaps best avoided.

Argument 2 (against): provision for the highly able will increase the gap between rich and poor

Schools cannot control the inequity of the society in which they function. If meeting the needs of the children in their care increases the gap between the richest and poorest in society, this is hardly their concern. Schools strive to do the best for their pupils and are expected to try and compensate for deficiencies and disadvantage wherever possible, not to hold children back. Until broader society is more equable, schools are likely to contribute unwillingly to social division. What schools tend to do within their own communities is assign provision on merit. As we have seen, this can be valuable where it is clear what is understood by merit.

Issues concerning the gap between rich and poor should not be the overriding concern of the school and should certainly not preclude provision for the able, nor act as sufficient reason to hold highly able children back.

Argument 3 (against): highly able children do not need special provision as their ability and background will assure their success

This common claim is grounded on two false assumptions, as clearly demonstrated by the evidence presented in Part One of this book. It is not true that high ability equals success – note the underachieving able. Neither is it true that all able children come from privileged backgrounds. It is a fact, though, that children from privileged homes demonstrate advanced knowledge of academic conventions and familiarity with the atmosphere and attitudes of school, so performing unfairly well in selection tests. Some will have been prepared for the examinations, and these are conducted in their first language and a familiar format. This suggests that entry to the programme should be made fair for all, including disadvantaged able pupils.[1] To help refute this argument, it is useful to summarise potential variations amongst pupils, albeit with a rather stereotypical, simplistic analysis:

1. average or low level of aptitudes   unfavourable environment
2. average or low level of aptitudes   favourable environment
3. high level of aptitudes   favourable environment
4. high level of aptitudes   unfavourable environment

Children in the first category have some programmes to help them and no teachers would wish to deny them this help and support. The second group have a certain advantage due to their background. It is often assumed that all able children fit the third group, but this is not the case. Pupils in the fourth are likely to exhibit unconventional behaviour or disaffection, because their home background is more likely to conflict with the values of the school and their high ability means they are acutely aware of this. Pupils from a favourable environment may also fall victim to disaffection, but are less likely to do so.

Children invited to attend in-school enrichment sessions are usually those who accede to school requirements – 'teacher pleasers' who work hard and are not disruptive. However, they often need no enrichment programmes to profit from schooling, as they are probably in a social situation that has benefited from successful education and family advantage. They should certainly be allowed to participate in enrichment activities and not be bored at school, but there are limited places on enrichment schemes and conventional pupils are normally rewarded with such opportunities in recognition of their hard work. Pupils who are able but who do not meet teacher expectations may well benefit more from these programmes, but are less likely to be selected. Enrichment could provide the chance to explore unusual ideas that stimulate motivation, or give them the freedom to explore their own strengths in a non-judgemental environment, away from peers who rate their abilities as 'uncool'.

The underlying understanding of high ability and a sense of fair distribution of resources are the factors that lead teachers to make decisions about just who should attend sessions. It is not necessarily lack of rigour that causes misdiagnosis of high ability. It could be the teacher's sense of merit that is perpetuating divisions between likely and unlikely achievers. Teachers' concern is often to reward conventional behaviour and task completion rather than encouraging less obviously talented pupils.[2]

George (1992) has produced a provocative list of characteristics of bright and gifted children. He shows how the bright child fits the conventional role of school pupil and provides less disruption in school than the gifted child:

Bright child	Gifted child
is interested	is highly curious
answers the questions	discusses in detail
knows the answers	asks the questions
top set	beyond the group
grasps the meaning	draws inferences
is alert	is keenly observant
completes the work	initiates projects
has good ideas	has unusual and silly ideas!
enjoys school	enjoys learning
good memory	good guesser
is pleased with learning	is highly critical
is receptive	is intense
learns easily	already knows
enjoys straightforward	
sequential presentation	thrives on complexity
enjoys peers	prefers adults or older pupils
absorbs information	manipulates information

This list is not exhaustive nor definitive but it does highlight some differences between children teachers tend to recommend for provision – 'bright children' – and those regularly referred to the Senco for some kind of investigation – certain 'gifted children'. My concern is for underachievers who often fit the non-conventional high ability profile.

Argument 4 (against): provision for the highly able offends against equality

Most teachers would subscribe to an ideal of equality and it seems that since able children already have an advantage through their aptitudes, it would be increasing inequality to provide anything extra for them. On the face of it, providing for the less able seems to be the rational way to move towards equality. It sounds like a sensible and fair ideal, but scratch the surface and complexities are revealed. In fact, there is no reason why everything should be equalised. It may well be that the distribution of resources and provision for pupils is unequal because so doing ultimately allows for greater fairness. I am specifically concerned with school policy here, as distinct from social policy, and consider it acceptable to pursue a non-egalitarian distribution of goods in order to achieve fairness. It is not the role of schooling to level the playing field.

> It is perfectly coherent to reject equality at the philosophical level, as a fundamental ideal, while arguing that, for other reasons, resources should be more equally distributed – perhaps much more equally distributed – than they are at present.
> *Swift, 2001:92*

In my experience, however, many teachers strive to be egalitarian, equating the term with fairness. Neither egalitarianism nor inegalitarianism are precise terms (Winch, 1996:128) and whilst initially it seems obvious to side with equality, on closer inspection, an anti-egalitarian 'middle position, based on a genuine commitment to meeting everyone's educational needs' seems preferable (White, 1994:180).

As we have seen, notions of equality require clarification. They are difficult to defend without firstly establishing the exact meaning of the key terms. I have shown that equality of resources could lead to unfairness and equality of outcome would put unnecessary pressure on pupils, or hold back the more able. Equality of opportunity is more complex, but still unclear. By lowering the bar, we could be sure that all pupils have the opportunity to achieve the basic minimum. This implies that where possibilities exist for only some pupils to train for district level sports, or learn the piano, it would be better for all to be denied the chance in the name of equality. This seems unfair and I agree with Brighouse's view that equality of opportunity is only a desirable ideal if qualified by other principles to stop it undermining more important values.

Arguments in favour of providing for the highly able
Argument 1 (for): academic excellence is intrinsically valuable

We generally consider academic success as being directly linked to job market options and as assuring financial success and stability. Able pupils who have no specific problems will be likely to reap the rewards of their high ability if they expend some effort and receive reasonable schooling, resulting in excellence, often translated into higher education, a graduate salary, or other similar, lucrative opportunities.

Some consider, however, that central subjects in traditional curricula are good in themselves and that excellence in these disciplines is its own reward, separate from the instrumental benefits just outlined. This view is presented by David Cooper:

> ... fundamental human concern in myriad areas of human practice – the concern with the attainment, in whatever field, of excellence; the concern that some should scale the heights.
> *1980:54*

This sets some people above others, potentially breeding resentment and leading to the view that programmes to help those of high ability are trying to provide a foot up into a different class stratum, with the implication that unselected pupils are somehow less valuable and can be left behind.

Patricia and John White effectively critique Cooper's ideas, demonstrating that he fails to 'show why excellence in the possession or pursuit of knowledge for its own sake should be a central educational aim'. They wonder if the excellence ideal would enjoy the same popularity if it resulted in a disadvantage in the job market. This is unlikely, suggesting that subjects are valued as means to ends. They also note that pushing children in one direction towards excellence can jeopardise well-being:

> ...Cooper has to show why their good is to have a lower priority than his excellence ideal: why, that is, their own good has to be sacrificed to knowledge (etc) for its sake. *1980:241*

Cooper's views focus on high ability children who are already demonstrating a certain level of achievement. Those with difficulties may be more expensive to teach and also subject to more risk factors, making them less likely to receive support than higher profile achieving pupils.

There is no good reason for the promotion of excellence for its own sake to take precedence over more widely distributed reasonable achievement or personal choice and well being.

Argument 2 (for): economic and social benefits accrue from focusing on the highly able, ensuring they achieve

There are two connected but slightly different aspects to this argument because economic and social benefits are both discrete and related. Encouraging excellence and high achievement will benefit a country's economy. This will be to everyone's advantage, as increased goods and wealth are redistributed to the rest of the population. However, this improvement is built on two questionable assumptions: fair distribution and able people achieving success. Firstly, higher productivity will not guarantee that others will benefit, until the redistribution of these goods is effectively managed. The second assumption – that the highly able will indeed turn their talents to economically productive uses – is also uncertain. Neither of these is under the jurisdiction of education *per se*, although schools do have a responsibility to deal with moral education for their pupils.

As noted, there is another way of considering meritocracy that links to the argument presented here and shows how there could be more goods for distribution.

> ... the efficiency-enhancing character of meritocracy makes it desirable – if people are allocated to positions (and the rewards that attach to them) according to merit (effort x talent) there will be more surplus, or social product, for us to redistribute. So

instead of having a desert-based case for meritocracy ... we have an efficiency-based case. *Brighouse, 2002:point 6*

Although this may be clearer than the complex desert notions, its success still rests on the two assumptions: efficient distribution, and the able making the best use of their abilities. Social goods are still placed above personal flourishing.

This could be accomplished in part by linking funding for expensive higher education to a certain amount of state service. Presently, many students sign up for costly courses and yet fail to translate training into practice. Without schemes that trace the state's investment in education to the productivity of the individual, it is difficult to guarantee value for money and a direct financial return on specific and targeted provision. Schemes that aim to do this are probably unworkable because of complex variables and the study of non-vocational subjects.

Some pursuits are less obviously linked to the economy or mainstream workplace, promoting a more contentious notion of what is useful for a society, such as funding for artists and musicians (even where the value of the art or music is not in question). Throughout history, key contributors to a nation's cultural development have fought for appreciation, have been unrecognised by their contemporaries, have struggled for survival. Their cultural and financial contribution may not be immediately apparent but it is equally valuable to that of people in more obvious fields of endeavour.

Moreover, it is difficult to separate the advantage to society from the advantage to the individual. If someone is supported in doing what they feel to be a worthwhile activity, this will impact on their own sense of well being. There is also the notion of protecting society. Unhappy able individuals can turn their abilities to activities that may harm society. Empirical evidence has shown that, although it is unusual, there is some susceptibility to mental health problems amongst the extremely highly able and also that disaffection in school can result in unlawful conduct. Provision for the able could therefore be considered as necessary protection from future problems.

Since economic and social benefits cannot be guaranteed, it is too tenuous a link to make such potential benefits the only reasons for providing for the able.

Argument 3 (for): special provision for the highly able is valuable because it can lead to a rise in general standards for all

There is some empirical evidence to support the contention that highly able pupils have a positive effect on their peers through positive role modelling and a strong classroom work ethic (Hallam and Ireson, 2001; Renzulli, 2000; Freeman, 1990). This is true only when able pupils are allowed the opportunity to be stretched through tasks undertaken with peers of the same ability, even if this needs to be provided outside the classroom.

Allowing children to excel can prevent behaviour problems and disaffection arising because they are bored. Pupils are also encouraged to remain in the maintained sector rather than leave to take up bursaries in independent schools which makes for a wider mix of pupils in schools.

Whether or not gifted provision can lead to a general rise in standards is an empirical question that should feature centrally in debates about the current government strategy. It seems that specialist schools are favoured in the UK, but international research indicates that this is not the best solution.

Argument 4 (for): all pupils are entitled to an education that takes them beyond the bare minimum

Were it sufficient to guarantee that all pupils emerge from schooling both literate and numerate, arguments about a minimal level of schooling would be acceptable. The notion that the state should only fund a minimum adequate education (Tooley, 2000) would require further educative experiences to be privately funded, while there might be sponsorship for poorer families. In order to run cost effective schools, the object would be for pupils to attain the required minimal levels as quickly as possible. Education authorities would then have met the targets and could slim down any other provision, or at least make a profit on children's further study. Our most able pupils might well leave as soon as they had met their targets.

Such as understanding of the goals of education is impoverished and inadequate. There should be some emphasis on the role of autonomy, which develops as pupils are allowed to express themselves effectively. This can only be accomplished in the kind of environment that treats individuals with respect and understanding, which in turn implies appropriate provision for the able as part of the student body. These ideas are in line with equality arguments.

In addition to the likely narrowness of an adequate minimum curriculum, there will obviously be problems of perpetuating the class system as families pick up provision where school leaves off. The inequalities that would result are criticised by Brighouse, who finds that resulting 'incentive-based inequalities' may be appropriate for adults but that 'these do not apply to the distribution of education among children' (2000:149). And it is difficult to identify the elements that would constitute an appropriate adequate minimum. Will this include social development through group activities, the development of dispositions and good work habits, and inspiration and enthusiasm for learning? These queries are raised in the Whites' paper (*op cit*:243) as it connects to notions of excellence.

Providing only a bare minimum will lead to inequality that is potentially damaging and it presents an impoverished model of education. Able pupils are unlikely to be intellectually challenged by a curriculum of this nature, especially where there are few extension tasks or very narrow teaching objectives. Teachers can also feel limited by a basic, restrictive curriculum.

Argument 5 (for): all pupils are entitled to an education based on their needs

All pupils have the same entitlements. These include basic numeracy and literacy, a fair chance in the job market, to be treated with respect, to have support for problems, to develop socially, personally and intellectually and to be challenged, stimulated and engaged. There is also a moral entitlement to ensure that any group is not unfairly disadvantaged by the distribution of goods.

A needs-based argument would seem counterproductive when trying to advocate for able pupils, as they seem to be unlikely candidates for provision outside of the curriculum. Some able pupils have additional needs, met (to a greater or lesser extent) by the school's legal obligation to provide support. High ability is not generally considered as a SEN and the statementing process and subsequent development of Individual Education Plans in such cases is usually left up to schools and LEAs to use or ignore, with only rough guidelines from the government.

If it could be shown that a pupil's development would be badly affected by being held back in class, there might be a case for extra provision to meet the emotional needs of a potentially disaffected pupil. This is usually only recognised when a child has already begun to exhibit anti-social behaviour, and the response is more likely to be punishment than a programme for high ability.

Needs are difficult to define in education, but I have distinguished here between instrumental and non-instrumental aspects of schooling in an attempt to make this easier. Instrumental or positional aspects of education tend to dominate discussions about what should and should not be provided. Brighouse, for example, focuses mainly on the positional aspects of education and, I think, places insufficient emphasis on other aspects (2000:115). Certainly the positional goods (that help compete for other goods) are likely to be greater for the high achieving able person. It is possible, however, that they are relatively unchallenged throughout their schooldays, not really benefiting from the intrinsic value that schooling can bring. Able underachievers fare less well, losing out on both fronts. They are both bored and in school, and they are mediocre or failures in the examination system.

All pupils are entitled to spend their compulsory schooling engaged in worthwhile and inspiring pursuits, undergoing a positive time in school. Pupils need to to engage with their learning and with the school they attend, to develop positive social relationships and to acquire a healthy self-image. Ensuring this would certainly involve changes to the schooling system, effectively differentiating curriculum and activities, providing additional and alternative classes, vertical grouping, individual work plans, teacher education, learning support and enrichment programmes.

There is nothing in what I am suggesting that necessarily implies that the highly able deserve or get additional benefits. Failing to make additional provision may, however, mean that efficiency related arguments are not satisfied. The connectedness of non-competitive and competitive goods in education creates problems. I am not arguing for access to additional benefits that are bound to accrue as the able improve their exam scores because they are getting a more stimulating and exciting educational experience. The able benefit from the value society places on their talent. I wish for a fairer society but not at the expense of sanctioning able children's experience at school being soul destroying and enthusiasm numbing. Provision for these children could be considered a way of equalising experience of personal challenge, allowing them to flourish through an enabling education.

Pupils are entitled to needs-based provision and should derive both instrumental and non-instrumental benefits from their education. For the able pupil, this may mean activities that go beyond the National Curriculum to ensure intellectual engagement and social situations that allow for the honest expression of the self. Pupils need a school ethos that encourages the bright pupil to shine and not force them to hide their talents deliberately.

Summary of arguments so far

In exploring common arguments in favour of and against provision for the able, I found the 'intrinsic value of excellence' notion to be elitist. There are only tenuous conclusions to be drawn from the contention that activities for the highly able will result in benefits for society through more and better economic and social goods. The effect of the able on other pupils is an empirical issue. It requires further investigation. The argument that all children need an education beyond the bare minimum applies to all pupils, not just the able, but it is unclear what should be put in and left out of such a programme of basic education. What would count as extra and what should be mandatory?

I have considered both instrumental and non-instrumental aspects of education in terms of the recipients' lifetime expected income and their lifetime expected flourishing and have concluded that education should be about more than examinations. Personal flourishing and fulfilment through learning are individual matters and individuals are encouraged to do their best, mainly for themselves, but with the understanding that people who are fulfilled are more likely to make a positive contribution to the system in which they find themselves.

The quality of schooling or learning experience is linked to the potential-achievement gap in a way that is particularly pertinent for the highly able. This has implications for equality, a concept that is rarely presented with clarity in the literature. Pupils should be measured by the relationship of their success to their potential achievement. There are difficulties associated with measuring potential, but it is often clear when students are failing to be appropriately challenged by their schoolwork. Should Astrid be achieving higher grades than Carlos, the obvious response is to try and help raise Carlos' results. But if Astrid is working well below her potential level of success, she may be bored, disaffected and frustrated. In terms of promoting flourishing, and of closing the potential-achievement gap, resources and effort should also be directed towards helping Astrid to improve her performance. This is not to advocate taking away from Carlos to ensure that Astrid flourishes, but the resource pot is unlikely to be big enough to cope with both children's needs. Decisions need to be made about how best to apportion resources, especially when Carlos may never reach Astrid's level in terms of grades. He is possibly able to flourish fully at his current level of achievement.

An illustration of the outcome of the commonly expressed arguments

To illustrate the arguments, let us take the example of two pupils, Oscar and Ella. One symbolises the reasons people intuitively reject high ability programming as perpetuating division and offending against equality, while the other exemplifies the path too often taken by able pupils when provision is inadequate.

Middle class Ella begins state school with an advantage over many of her peers because of attending private nursery. Her well-educated parents value schooling and provide a home life enriched with museum visits, educational computer games, books and general knowledge. When tested for the gifted programme, Ella is nervous and mindful of her performance. Ella naturally shares her parents' values and once she is successfully installed in the enrichment programme she continues to make full use of her well-ingrained work ethic, achieving reasonable grades. Her friendship group is drawn from highly able peers in her class and their shared interests and study approaches are echoed through the high expectations of teachers and pupils. Barring disasters in her personal life, Ella's academic success is pretty much assured.

Oscar is able and interested, but his parents cannot secure him a nursery place. He is happy and safe with his child-minder, but seems to prefer the company of adults and older children to those of his own age. When Oscar begins school, he is all at sea. Despite the activity and freedom, he fails to bond with the other pupils, spending much of the day enjoying the book corner, the quietest part of the open plan room. He completes activities quickly, but the short-cuts he creates to finish tasks earn him a reputation for carelessness. Oscar applies his same rushed attitude to the test for the gifted programme, answering the oral questions impatiently and emerging as a borderline candidate. His teachers consider he would benefit from staying in normal class to improve his 'slap-dash' attitude and allow a 'more deserving hard worker' the place.

Oscar becomes increasingly bored with school, retreating further into a world of his own and paying less and less heed to his parents' pleas to take classwork more seriously. He bides his time, kicks his heels, keeps out if trouble and leaves school as soon as he can, with an undistinguished clutch of qualifications and a sense of disappointment.

Equality of provision should bring Oscar's opportunities up to those of Ella's but not deny Ella the chance to participate in activities that bring her challenge. It would be unethical to hamper Ella by using her background as a reason to disallow her enrichment. She works hard so she merits the opportunity to benefit from the enrichment programme. Oscar also deserves to have a valuable time in school. He should be challenged, not bored. Denial of provision based on a notion of his lack of desert is unfair, largely because his behaviour is being misinterpreted. He is indeed 'lazy' and 'slapdash' and these are not qualities to be praised. He has, however, been unable to develop the disposition for a positive work ethic through a combination of factors beyond his control. Why then should he be penalised?

Conclusion

All children should be provided with an enabling education with sufficient resources to allow the development of their talents to a high level, particularly when there is a significant discrepancy between their potential and their performance. This is true even where potential achievement exceeds expected requirements. A clearer and fairer way of determining what it is fair to do for the able is to aim for some kind of equality of quality of learning, or equality of challenge.

References

1   In the Philippines, there is difficulty encouraging children to take up programmes due to the sense of fairness across families; it is considered wrong to 'favour' one sibling over another. Open access programmes were therefore set up, with no entry qualifications. Students were expected only to attend with regularity. The sessions were very popular and results demonstrated that achievement was raised for all pupils. (Wu *et al*, 2000)

2   I am not suggesting that teachers only 'like' conventional pupils, but that school structures work in these pupils' favours. Teachers sometimes emphasise behaviour and self-control as key factors for choice of provision and although this may be practical, it lacks pedagogical validity.

5

Equality of challenge

A defeated child: Nina, age 5, Year 2

Nina seemed unusually serious and sad, though she had a happy home life and good relationships with her siblings, parents and friends. Nina's parents were aware of her unusual abilities and did their best to keep her stimulated by making books and learning experiences available. They tried to avoid making a fuss of her abilities, wanting to help her develop a healthy social circle and self-concept. Nina initially enjoyed the experience of her Nursery class, but soon grew frustrated at waiting for her peers to catch her up. At least in the Nursery she was able to play once she had completed set tasks.

As Nina moved to Reception, she continued to complete tasks well but her interactions with classmates and teachers diminished. The school suspected a problem, but the psychologist they called in diagnosed 'boredom' and charged the teachers with the responsibility of keeping her busy with meaningful tasks.

She skipped Year One and once she was separated from her friends she became even more despondent. Nina coped with her work easily and soon became the first in her class to finish set tasks and extra work. Her parents noted her increasing silence at home. At school she became withdrawn and stopped communicating with teachers and children except for responding politely to direct questions.

Do you think you're good at learning?

Nina: I don't know. (Long pause.) I am quick at work. Then I sit on the book cushion and think about why I am quick at work.

Why do you do that?

I have to do that because that's what you must do if you have read all the books.

Introduction

We have seen that all children should be provided with an enabling education that offers sufficient resources to allow the development of their talents to a high level, particularly when there is a significant discrepancy between their potential and their performance. This is true even where potential achievement exceeds expected requirements.

Providing equality of challenge, or equality of quality of learning for all pupils, should be a key factor in schooling. Able pupils in particular are likely to need provision beyond the National Curriculum to ensure such stimulation (Koshy and Casey, 1998). While there is a statutory requirement to attend school, there is a moral obligation for schools to ensure that pupils are not wasting their time. They need to be engaged in their learning and this can only happen when they find activities challenging. Even the most determined of us can only sustain a certain amount of motivation for simple tasks that lack intrinsic value.

Deciding on a universally applicable definition of challenge is a challenge in itself, but activities should be appropriately pitched for all pupils. Ensuring a good match between task and ability may well require increased resources, training and facilities. Pupils must move at their own intellectual pace, or as near to this as is practically possible, regardless of whether that pace is 'normal' for their age.

Some people seem to have the potential to display excellence in a broad range of pursuits and it would seem unfair to provide for their development in all these fields, especially where those who have a narrower range of abilities are not provided with whatever tools they may need for success. But it is not a matter of choice between 'all for one' and 'none for some'.

Brighouse states that equality of experience as a principle for establishing education policy cannot be ensured. We can only consider equality of opportunity, or even a minimising of inequality of educational opportunity (Brighouse, 2000:149). I contend that pupils are entitled to some kind of equality in their school experience; that they are entitled to more than the minimising of inequality of educational opportunity. We can try to ensure this through consideration of the quality of teaching and the level of challenge with which they are presented.

Practical application of this notion is discussed in Part Three, with particular reference to critical thinking skills programmes as appropriate challenge.

The nature and importance of challenge

It is impossible to create a single prescription for challenge for all, although it seems obvious that an interesting subject area and tasks of a suitable level would provide stimulation. Challenge is not a new concept, although it is easy to lose sight of its importance. It should be a focus above outcomes and targets. It should be an explicit aspect of schooling.

Challenge is intimately bound up with motivation and this can be intrinsic or extrinsic. Superficial external rewards will not ensure continued interest in an area of study. Children need to derive genuine intrinsic motivation from the task in hand and this cannot always be ensured merely through the subject areas found in school curricula. Workshop sessions for the highly able cover a wide range of unusual issues, hoping to stimulate as many interests as possible. That is not to say that sessions lack depth. There may be extended study where appropriate. Open-minded children will come away from sessions with a broader range of interests, or an appreciation of the depth of a topic.

Once it is clear that the subject in question is stimulating to the child or potentially interesting to them, it is important to attain the right balance in setting tasks. The level of difficulty should be pitched to avoid frustration or boredom. When a task is too easy, children become bored, sometimes even refusing to undertake what they perceive as pointless. If a task is too complex, without any obvious entry points, it can be too frustrating even to begin. Children need to feel some level of competence in order to motivate them 'to exercise and elaborate their abilities' (Freeman, 2000:577).

Cognitive challenge was well described by Vygotsky in terms of the Zone of Proximal Development (ZPD), and by Piaget and other developmentalists. They used the term 'cognitive dissonance'. Dissonance in this sense describes sufficient challenge to ensure optimum learning. The ZPD defines what can currently be achieved with support, and the move toward what will soon be accomplished without help. Vygotsky recommended the support of an adult or more capable peer, but this can also be provided through written or recorded instruction. Many able pupils find computer technology ideal in terms of being able to control the amount of assistance they require.

Challenge must include a risk of failure. Generally children choose tasks just a little harder than their previous successes, as the impulse to improve is intuitive for children who have a good sense of their abilities. Watching children in an adventure playground demonstrates this. Children are rarely injured because they attempt a task that is way beyond their capabilities. Children do not repeat the same level task endlessly; they do so only until they feel confident enough to move to the next level.

Teachers often know perfectly well how to provide challenge by designing tasks that capture children's imagination. The palpable buzz that results from a busy class of children engaged in sustained concentration and interested enquiry is instantly recognisable. But for a variety of reasons, teachers cannot always provide this level of engagement. Sometimes it is too time-consuming to plan activities, or too complex to provide appropriate resources, but often there are just too many competing issues in the classroom to allow for the kind of atmosphere that promotes excited learning.

The dangers of ignoring challenge

Potential problems caused by too much time without challenge are noted by Montgomery:

> ... boredom and lack of cognitive challenge in the daily curriculum is playing a more significant role in causing pupils across the ability range to become disaffected than was originally suspected.[...] more pupils, including the highly able and the more creative, are rejecting such 'schooling' and are switching off. We now have the situation where the National Curriculum and the methods by which it is taught have especially not led to a stimulating and educative experience for the gifted and talented. *2000:130-131*

More pervasive problems can result from the able being habitually bored. If they come to expect to be bored, this negative attitude can infect other areas of their lives, as they generalise the boredom to other experiences. They can also become disruptive:

> The gifted, like any others, need the enjoyable stimulation of variety, and the excitement of playing with ideas. So, when lessons are too easy, they lose the satisfaction of tackling and resolving problems. To compensate, they may deliberately provoke disturbance, either in their own minds or among others in the classroom, just to taste the spice of stimulation. *Freeman, 1997:488*

We are generally able to find our own level of challenge and the able child in the classroom is capable of doing so if the materials available are flexible enough to match their needs. I doubt whether any research could find the perfect formula for creating challenge, as it inevitably varies from one individual to the next. However, some factors could be determined. Key ingredients are likely to be:

• intrinsically interesting subjects

• well-thought out, systematic development of ideas

• the real possibility of both failure and success.

Conclusion

I have defended provision for the able on the grounds that even though provision cannot (and need not) be the same for everyone, there must be equality of value in the education provided. There will be inequality of outcome, resources and opportunities, but there must also be more than a minimum safety net.

Provision for the able does not need to be elitist, although it is likely that the achievement gap will increase between the most able who have no problems and the rest of the school population. The alternatives – ignoring able underachievers and holding back able high achievers – are unacceptable. Disaffected able pupils and those with learning problems should be helped and the resultant rising tide could elevate general achievement. It is possible that developed talent can be harnessed to help meet the needs of the least advantaged through increased economic and social productivity. How best to do this is a matter for research, as is the empirical question concerning the extent of the effect on other pupils in school of provision for the able.

We should not have to hamper able pupils in order to equalise their prospects. That the societal playing field is uneven is not a good enough reason to make schooling a waste of time for able advantaged children. Society must adapt to allow all participants to do their best. It is the distribution of income and wealth that is at fault, not the educational ideal of striving to meet children's needs.

Pursuing excellence for its own sake constitutes insufficient grounds to provide for the able, but meeting individual needs is a compelling reason for doing so. Pupils should be presented with challenge every day and while I am an ardent advocate for the able and more specifically underachievers, my views are tempered with a realistic attitude to the practical restrictions that are likely.

It would be impossible to fund all the activities in which the able might excel and so choices need to be made so that the most challenging or useful are selected. It may be that meeting children's needs results in some people costing the system more than others. If they are not able, fine. If they are able, fine.

It is fair to do something for highly able children. It is unfair to do nothing.

PART THREE
What should we provide for the able?

6

Common responses to the needs of the highly able

An impulsive child: Charlie, age 5, Year 3

On day one of school, each pupil was given a pencil, for which they were responsible. Pencils had been pooled in Year 2 but now children were to look after their own things. It was part of the process of moving up to 'big school'. In their pristine, just-too-big uniforms, the children were attentive to the symbolic significance of their new responsibility. Charlie was sitting at the table of children who were the first to receive shiny new pencils. I had barely reached the second table when there was a loud crack and a collective gasp. Charlie wriggled. He had managed to snap his pencil clean in half.

And so it continued. For a full year, this very bright and capable child demonstrated time and again that personal control was beyond him at this stage. Even our informal and relaxed classroom was too restrictive and rule bound, making every day a struggle and every set task a battle of wills. Charlie's written work never lived up to his obvious promise and, while he continued to offer great ideas and unusual excellent oral responses, he produced little in his exercise books and manifested no learning problems to explain his lack of writing.

Do you think you're good at learning?

Charlie: Only electronics [not taught at school] and maths and not reading. Also you can learn from TV and books and the Internet and teachers don't have all the answers. I am not good at cursive (writing). I like games, but I am a butterfingers and Mr Coltrane said I am a curate's egg, which is good in bits. Are you good at learning?

Highly able pupils do merit provision, so what can be done in mainstream school settings? What is the role of the teachers and what qualities do they need? Pupils have different abilities, interests and motivations and it is difficult to cater for their diverse needs. The highly able are generally low on the list of priorities because it is assumed that they can manage without help or support. I have demonstrated that in many cases this is not true. Research supports the need for provision not as icing-on-the-cake elitist indulgence, but as necessary for all schools. Able children are seldom well understood and they are often set inappropriate tasks.

> Some educationalists have included able pupils in the category of newly disadvantaged groups.[...] A typical sample of research findings is: In the case of the most able groups the work was considerably less well-matched than for average and less able groups (HMI, 1978:81). High attainers were under-estimated on 40% of tasks assigned to them (Bennett *et al*, 1984:215). In the majority of schools the expectations of very able pupils are not sufficiently high (HMI, 1992:28). *Eyre 1997:1*

I outline three common approaches to supporting the able, acceleration, enrichment and extension and then highlight issues that able underachievers raise. The chapter closes with a discussion of the two most important aspects of provision, differentiation and teachers relinquishing control.

General approaches: acceleration

Acceleration involves placing a pupil in a different year group from his or her chronological peers, mostly skipping one or two years, and occasionally making even larger jumps. Acceleration is sometimes accompanied by rather dramatic local media coverage. Such sensationalism is partly responsible for the common knee-jerk response that acceleration is likely to be harmful. When examination results are made public in the UK, tabloid and local papers present pictures of young pupils with clutches of GCSEs and sometimes A-levels to rival those achieved by 16 and 18-year-olds. The timbre of such coverage sometimes suggests that the child's welfare may be at stake (Freeman, 1983). Praise for astounding achievement is tempered with an emphasis on the abnormality of the child. More detailed profiles combine admiration for achievement with concern for the future.[1]

Acceleration is in danger of being a hot-housing showcase. With schools increasingly expected to promote themselves, children can be made to jump through hoops for the glory of the school rather than for their own development. It may not necessarily be harmful to encourage children to sit such exams at an early age, but there is the possibility of burn-out or of becoming bored with consequent learning. Pupils who have mastered an A-level at 14 are not necessarily equipped to make the most of a degree course. Benefits accrued from accelerating a pupil so they experience intellectual challenge can be outweighed by social and emotional concerns. An age gap of several years can affect children with differing severity at different points in a school career.

Having found success with this strategy, Gross introduces the notion of 'radical acceleration', defined as 'several grade-skips spaced appropriately through the student's school career'. She reports that nine of 58 subjects have entered university at ages between 11-16 and that 'all are experiencing high levels of academic success and full social lives' (Gross, 2000:189).

> It cannot be sufficiently emphasised, however, that the problems of social isolation, peer rejection, loneliness and alienation which afflict many extremely gifted children arise not out of their exceptional intellectual abilities but as a result of society's response to them. *p188*

This may be so, but the issue is still real. Until societal changes allow for this problem to be solved, children will need to deal with the difficulties that acceleration bring and for some this would be a counter-productive strategy. Gross, however, would consider overcoming these obstacles to be worthwhile and this is understandable in light of these quotations from two of her subjects:

> I'm sorry it was necessary to do something that was so unusual at the time, but I certainly don't regret doing it. The alternative – staying with age peers – would have been intolerable.

...bleakly encapsulated his life in the heterogeneous classroom in a single word: 'Hell'.

Sometimes acceleration works very smoothly. If the pupil is mature enough to mix well with peers and the change to more challenging work has a positive effect on self-esteem, it can be the perfect response. Theorists and teachers generally agree that each case should be considered on its own merits as the individual and their context will largely determine success. There are also support strategies that can help ease the process. For some pupils, the social aspect of acceleration is entirely unproblematic. Finding that peers have problems understanding their ideas and language, able pupils often befriend older children and adults. Apparent outsiders can fit in when accelerated, and their off-putting quirky nature becomes comfortably contextualised and problem free. Sometimes this happens when a child moves to a school with a different ethos from the last. This was Stan's experience. His unusual rhyming and word play had made it difficult for him to make friends, but when he moved to a more academic school he flourished, mainly because he started studying classics and languages such as Latin and Greek, in which his word play was of great help.

Judging when to stop accelerating and continuing with effective differentiation can be difficult, especially when pupils are still well ahead of their classmates. The practicalities of keeping pupils interested once they have completed the curriculum at an early stage can be insurmountable. If the acceleration is not coordinated with the next phase of provision, the whole project can be negated and result in repetition. Recent research has already indicated that much of Year 7 in secondary schools serves as little more than a repeat of the material covered in Year 6.[2] It is important to begin with assessments that allow pupils to show what they already know, and allow exemption from work already completed and understood.

As the main concern with acceleration is to ensure the development of positive social relationships, a valuable strategy is to allow the pupils to mix vertically in different settings, including clubs and classes. A common problem for the accelerated child is physical education, where being much smaller than peers can make sporting activities difficult. Contrary to the stereotype, highly able children tend to be good all-rounders. But for Miles this was a problem when he was accelerated. Other pupils who were threatened by his high achievements in maths and English exploited his rather poor football skills because of his age and inexperience. Being two years younger than classmates and also rather short, his unusual abilities, coupled with his size, made him a target for bullying.

Another strategy would be to make a more radical move and abandon the idea of traditional class age-groupings. This would stop the able pupil being seen as the odd one out and might help promote more harmonious social integration. Acceleration is the strategy most affected by the institutional framework. It is an exaggeration of setting and streaming which requires considerable flexibility and teamwork if it is to work.

General approaches: enrichment

Enrichment provides breadth of learning by exposing pupils to a wide range of different activities and ideas, helping them to see connections, discover interests and talents and develop different skills, knowledge and understanding. Schools may strive to offer pupils a range of activities that do not relate directly to the curriculum and provide opportunities they may not otherwise be afforded due to their economic or home background. But this is not a kind of compensatory educational strategy as much as a way of allowing children opportunities to express their abilities.

To prevent activities becoming a shallow or meaningless 'pick and mix' of fun which lacks depth or coherence, a well-considered selection of activities should be ensured, with access as part of an explicit whole-school policy. Teachers need support in referring and recommending pupils to attend sessions. They can only do this when they understand the available provision. For example, children with aptitudes in mathematics may be encouraged to learn strategic games, such as chess, or investigate astronomy, and be encouraged to develop their academic mathematics through competitions and examination syllabi.

Organised out-of-schools activities have increased notably, partly as a response to the perceived danger of letting children play unsupervised in public parks and streets and partly as a result of children needing to build curriculum vitae for entrance to competitive schools. The concept of the 'hyper-parent' has recently surfaced as a concern.[3] Children are ferried from tap-class to T'ai Chi, to private tutors and French classes, leaving them little down time. Some schools and workshops are activity-led and consist of like-minded individuals who have a shared interest such as sewing, country dancing or bridge. These offer intrinsic rewards rather than certificates or improved grades. Others are competitive, or designed to maximise classroom performance in each Key Stage. There are independent school Common Entrance exam crammer courses for prestigious 13-plus entry to independent schools and there are courses to remediate problems. The internet has allowed people with shared interests to meet up 'virtually', which is of tremendous use to able pupils who want to research an area in detail. (Concerns about internet child safety are addressed by school gateways.)[4]

Activities designed specifically for the highly able tend to be more child-led; outcomes and subject area are considered less important than the opportunity for challenge. At out-of-school enrichment courses, a group of children attend residential or day sessions, opting from a selection of planned workshops spanning a wide range of topics. There are opportunities for social mixing and trying out new ideas and projects. As all pupils are selected for high ability, there is no need to wait for any of the group to catch up. Small group sizes allow staff to spend more time with each pupil and the relaxed atmosphere with no pressures of tests, targets or statutory activities helps develop more open and creative responses to set tasks. Pupils' behaviour is rarely an issue and it is possible to allow a certain laxness in rules, as the children's motivation ensures on-task and focused work. The children police one another when required, and the strength of feeling that comes from tackling a group task together encourages a responsible attitude to working.

School and family activity days allow parents to share in their children's enthusiasms. Activities should also be available for parents at their own level, to present a positive model of adult learning. The family that can appreciate one another's interests is likely to offer a positive atmosphere that encourages children to pursue projects and ideas as they wish. In my experience of such days, teachers, parents and children reported learning a great deal about their own and others' abilities.

General approaches: extension

Extension entails going beyond the basic prescribed tasks. The model used at the planning stage generally requires teachers to outline (a) minimum tasks, (b) recommended further tasks, and (c) optional extension tasks that able pupils can undertake as extension of the basic class activity. This 'must, could, should' approach is preferable to adding extra activities as children finish prescribed work. Ensuring continuity and progression is 'far more valuable than bolt-on, one-off extension ideas' (Eyre, 1997:40-1).

Extending pupils beyond the level expected for their chronological age can be difficult. Able infants have found themselves in the position of having read every storybook in the library. These 'hyperlexic' pupils are then directed to fiction that may have themes inappropriate to their emotional maturity – material designed mainly for young teenagers. There are problems too, for the teachers as there may be no available materials for the next stage in the relevant subject. Next year's teacher will not thank her colleague for using up all the texts and plans intended for her upcoming group.

Some subject areas lend themselves to extension better than others. Literature can be problematic when it introduces themes children find awkward to discuss even when the mechanics of literary criticism are within their grasp. Similarly, musical performance often requires a sensitivity beyond the child because they have too little experience upon which to draw. Mathematics and languages, however, are appropriate fields for extension.

Pupils inevitably demonstrate a wide range of abilities and this affects the mechanics of running a school and meeting curricular demands. It makes practical sense to minimise difference and group children loosely, teaching them with the same materials. Extension is only practically workable where there are very small classes and where teachers can be extremely flexible.

Summary of strategies

Acceleration is appropriate for the socially mature individual and where there are structures in place to support the decision. Radical acceleration is only useful in a small minority of cases, but can sometimes be the perfect solution. Sometimes home schooling could provide a suitable response, or a specific specialist school for example where the talent is in music. Extension requires a great deal of flexibility on the part of the school and can be too impractical to offer a real solution. Differentiation is a part of all the strategies. Enrichment emerges as the best all-inclusive strategy (if one strategy alone needs to be recommended). It has the potential to involve a wide range of pupils and it fits easily into school structures so that although aimed primarily at the able, other pupils can benefit too.

Which techniques may help all pupils, and which are only appropriate for the able can be summarised as follows:

Uniquely appropriate for gifted
acceleration
career education (girls)
ability grouping
high level curriculum
differential programming

Effective with gifted and general education
enrichment
inquiry, discovery, problem solving and creativity
professional end products as standards
microcomputers
*Gallagher, 2000:688 adapting Shore and Delcourt, 1996
and echoed by Moon and Rosselli, 2000:505*

This list suggests that a flexible and open curriculum which provides discovery, problem solving and creativity is more important than ability grouping – the common response. If provision can help the able as well as other pupils, this method should obviously be adopted wherever possible.

Rather than than relying on a single strategy, a range of factors should be taken into account. These include general pedagogy, incorporating consideration of classroom management issues such as grouping of children, outside support such as clubs, and overall school organisation. Curriculum content and assessment are important, but the key factor is likely to be how teachers interact with individual students.

Highly able underachievers

Of the approaches detailed here, all can be useful for the able underachiever depending on their particular situation. Finding good practice for the able underachiever is a useful guide for working with all pupils, as it necessitates understanding the principles and practice of catering for all individual needs a teacher is likely to meet (except for highly specialised education for people with severe physical disabilities and sensory impairments. See Winstanley, 2003). Defining principles of good practice in this way allows for pedagogy that helps not only pupils with SEN but all pupils, because individual needs are more explicitly taken into consideration.

An example of this would be classroom management techniques, such as minimising disruption and distraction. This is essential for pupils with Attention Deficit/Hyperactivity Disorder (AD/HD) but is helpful to all pupils as it assists their concentration. Pupils with visual dyslexia are well served by particular use of colour on whiteboards and handouts, pupils with dyspraxia appreciate an uncluttered spatial layout and those with Asperger's Syndrome require unambiguous instruction. All these techniques help the other pupils to work more effectively, partly through the clarity they provide and partly through the calmer classroom environment that reduces or prevents behaviour problems associated with children with learning difficulties.

Legislation has not been very helpful. The introduction of the five-step Code of Practice (1994) included guidelines for helping children whose difficulties are not severe enough to warrant a 'statement of need' but who still require support. 'Statementing' was finally clarified in the 1996 Education Act and is continually updated. However, the use of statements for enshrining the needs of the able is still rare as '...able pupil provision falls into the 'guidance category' and is not legally binding' (Eyre, 1997:110). The Code emphasises partnership support, involving outside agencies and parents, as well as requiring all schools to publish a whole-school special needs policy. Ofsted inspectors can use the Code of Practice to assess schools' approach to coping with children with complex needs. As a result of this attention, the needs of the able pupils are beginning to be highlighted, and the role of the Special Educational Needs Coordinator (Senco) reinforced and clarified.

Defining SEN has always been rather difficult. Parameters change as society shifts its interpretation of need and support. In 2003, Montgomery presented a broad range of 'dually exceptional' children, including children with Down's Syndrome and noted that high ability can accompany any of the areas identified in the SEN categorisation of 2001. The UK is moving towards inclusive practice, partly in response to assumptions of the Salamanca Statement[5] 'that all children's educational needs can be satisfied, more or less, within the regular classroom in a mixed-ability setting' (Persson, 2000:724). Whilst teachers may welcome less segregated provision, they need flexibility to be able to cope with a widening range of needs. They see the National Curriculum as restrictive in this regard, as they are unable to adopt their own curriculum initiatives that might more readily address the needs of 'pupils with problems' (Garner, 1999:100).

The phrase 'able misfit' was coined by Kellmer-Pringle in 1970, to describe pupils with an unusually large gap between potential and achievement. This is an inappropriate label for contemporary discussions, in part because the stereotype of the underachieving able pupil has been discredited, but also because it is now read as a simplistic expression which takes no account of reasons for lack of achievement (Kerr, Colangelo and Gaeth, 1988).

Research has recently allowed for more comprehensive understanding of the able underachiever. They may be:

- coasters – children who achieve reasonably but expend little effort

- high fliers – children who achieve highly and work hard

- other categories – disruption in class and disaffection.
  Wallace, 2000

- underachiever – participates in classroom activities; lack of achievement reflects a tangible difficulty

- non-producer – not really invested in the classroom structure; does not share group aims of individual success and collective accomplishment. *Freeman, 1998*

There are also the invisible able pupils who are not outstanding to the casual eye. They can convince teachers they are reasonable workers, achieving appropriately average grades for their pedestrian work and not being disruptive or making trouble. On closer inspection it is clear they are completing set tasks to a reasonable standard in an exceptionally short time. The rest of the allocated time is spent in apparently fruitless tasks; over-sharpening pencils, gazing outside, balancing rulers precariously on their desks, walking surreptitiously around the classroom by the longest route in a quest for vital equipment, etc. Such pupils show up as highly able on conventional psychological intelligence and creativity tests (eg. AH1, WISC-R and Urban) but are ranked as average or below average by teachers and self-identify as not enjoying school. Teachers mistakenly but understandably interpret this average work as reflecting pupils' average ability.[6]

Teachers coping with highly able children: differentiation and relinquishing control

Teachers aim to recognise and cater for individual differences. This is an essential teaching tactic which lies at the heart of effective classroom practice, but it can be a difficult task. Eyre describes true differentiation as an 'aspiration', but emphasises that this 'does not negate the need to strive for improvement' (1997:38-9). Concern over effective differentiation preoccupies many teachers. It is defined thus:

Teaching things differently according to observed differences among learners (Westwood, 2001:5). Differentiation strategies can be applied to:

- teaching approach
- content of the curriculum
- assessment methods
- classroom organisation

- student grouping
- teachers' interactions with individual students. *Westwood, 2003:202*

For example, in learning about the water cycle, all children could complete a worksheet to show understanding, but they would have gleaned the information from different sources. In this differentiation by resources, groups could be given information in diverse formats: pre-written, pictorial, video or audio, or through free access to the library or internet. Tasks would be different for each group; perhaps providing more effective and directed differentiation than giving the whole group the same introduction and expecting written responses of varying depth and sophistication.

Differentiation can be achieved by the 'three-worksheet phenomenon'. Lessons are taught using three different worksheets: one with a great deal of writing, one with a larger font size and a graphic, and one with plenty of pictures. Pupils assess themselves by their assigned worksheets. Highly able children are expected to be capable readers and are thus given the first worksheet. Less able pupils are given the third worksheet – the one with all the pictures – and their tasks are likely to involve only the basic concepts. But what about the highly able pupil with reading problems?

The phrase 'maximising potential' has been creeping into the literature, partially replacing differentiation. Notwithstanding the irritation that new vocabulary can cause, reframing differentiation in this way could help teachers focus on getting the best from each individual rather than trying to rank them according to difference or worrying about having a range of activities available. This is closer to the approach implied by using Individual Education Plans (IEP) tailored to meet specific needs (Code of Practice, 1994). In cases where pupils have an SEN along with high ability, the focus for support is often the area of difficulty. In such cases, IEPs would be the optimum response, as group sessions make differentiation very complex. This could also meet the government's latest recommendation for personalised learning.

However, with able underachievers even in one-to-one consultations, the need for appropriate challenge can still be overshadowed by remediation. Billie, the child with dysgraphia, exemplified this.

She was often required to copy out chunks of text to help rehearse letter formation. This is a fairly soul-destroying activity for any individual, and with able pupils, dysgraphia is often caused by the need to write fast enough to capture ideas, and does not mean they do not understand about letter formation. A better tactic than slowing down the mechanics of writing in order to help legibility, would be to help the pupil find an alternative way of recording ideas. Instead of pages of linear longhand, the child could use notes, diagrams, tape recording or shorthand. Teachers could then impress upon the pupil the importance of legibility in communicating ideas, which they could accomplish by using the notes as a basis for the response to the set task. This allows the pupil to record their thoughts at their own pace and is a better way to demonstrate understanding of their needs, showing respect for their ideas and helping to build practical, transferable strategies. There is still a place for penmanship sessions, but these can be differently and narrowly focused.

An obvious response to problems caused by differentiation would seem to be reducing the range of ability in any one class by streaming, setting or selective schooling. Variation is not as marked but will still exist and require differentiation. Teachers' expertise in meeting these needs comes from a combination of factors including subject knowledge and a good understanding of pupil needs.

Selecting the right kind of pedagogy can imply a shift in power in the teaching situation, and different situations call for an adaptive role from teachers. Sometimes a firm lead and clearly established boundaries are required, but there are also occasions where pupils need freedom and a loose structure in order to flourish. The highly able have deep interests in valid areas they can pursue in independent studies and curiosity can be re-ignited through a shift in the set task.[7] Teachers are often reluctant to negotiate with pupils, as this might indicate that they are losing control of the direction of learning, or unfairly favouring some pupils. But this is not so: they are responding to pupils' needs by differentiating tasks based on collaborative assessment, in partnership with the pupils.

To illustrate: take the battles with Louis over homework in Religious Education. He had failed to complete weekly homework for RE for three months. In my capacity as Senco, I was asked to help iron out the problem of Louis' lack of co-operation (not to ensure that he was being challenged). The teacher's plan was to consider differences within Christianity and there were a series of tasks to complete over several weeks, with an identical task for the whole class. These tasks all had the same structure: research a denomination of Christianity, find a representative church and write a few paragraphs on the layout and architecture, demonstrating how this linked with the nature of the religion. Louis was horrified at the thought of having to complete four rather similar drawings over four weeks and described the task as 'dull, dull ... unbelievably dull'. I asked him what he was planning to do, since he was required to complete some homework and was already in serious trouble for general non-compliance. Avoiding the task was not an option, unless he wanted to push the school into considering exclusion, as he was already on report in several other subjects, mainly for 'being cheeky'. (In my classroom observations I would have disputed this interpretation in a number of cases, though not all.)

Louis made a suggestion for the RE homework. He would draw a basic church shape and then use transparent overlays to illustrate the features that would mark out the differences in belief, ritual and emphasis. He was rather excited about this original approach and got started immediately. The work he produced was of a high standard and his annotations were far more detailed and well-researched than the short paragraphs that even the high achieving pupils produced. Louis had completed two of the overlays when the RE teacher said: 'No. I have to put my foot down. It's not about doing what you want, Louis. It's about doing as you are told. You've got away with a whole term just mucking about and now you've shown you can work, you must get on with the homework I set just like everyone else. You're nothing special.'

Louis stopped working and went back to avoidance tactics. He was particularly angry with me for letting him down. I had assured him the teacher was open to negotiations, but I was wrong. She changed her mind and started seeing him as a threat to the smooth running of her classroom, fearing accusations of being too lenient. Louis had begun to change his opinion of her, but he dropped back into accusing her of being unimaginative and narrow-minded. What Louis had suggested was a perfectly valid differentiated task, meeting the learning objectives of the curriculum and probably also suitable for other class members.

Teacher-pupil relationships involve shifts in control, as trust builds and pupils demonstrate their motivation and work ethic. Negotiating homework will better allow children to see the value of what they are being asked to study, as aims and goals are made explicit. Most highly able pupils are capable of making suggestions and decisions about how best they can achieve set goals. With pupils having control over their learning, teachers take on more of a supervisory role, helping, guiding and facilitating, rather than prescribing.

It is difficult to allow a few pupils such freedom while the rest of the group are set more prescriptive tasks. Dealing with such complex management is possible only where there is trust and understanding between pupils and teachers and where it is understood that it is not favouritism but pupils' needs that are the reason for these approaches. Highly able children must be seen to be working hard and not 'getting away with doing nothing'. If they are thought to be coasting while classmates are struggling this will be a recipe for resentment.

Using able pupils as learning mentors is another strategy. The mentor pupil, if accelerated, will initially have to build friendships, and a mentor system can help with this. Mentors who are not accelerated can get to know peers who may find them difficult to understand in ordinary class situations. At the same time, the pupils they are helping have an opportunity to work with someone who can give them full attention and who is close in age. This method can work well if handled by a sensitive teacher who makes a thoughtful pairing, where both pupils can benefit from meaningful personal discussions about work that can seldom be managed in a whole class situation. Teachers' roles are altered, not lessened.

Able pupils have clear views on the characteristics of their teachers they most admire and unsurprisingly prefer humour, creativity and curiosity.[8] The preferences invite a trusting teacher-pupil relationship and this can require the teacher to relinquish some control, acceding to pupils' suggestions. In general, pupils appreciate teachers who provide appropriately differentiated tasks and trust and respect pupils enough to negotiate work tasks – within reason.

Conclusion

Provision for the able is currently patchy and lacks coherence. Of particular concern is the lack of attention given to able under-achievers, who miss out even where provision is available. To help overcome this, high ability could benefit from being reframed as a SEN, but only if teachers are properly equipped to deal with high ability issues. Account also needs to be taken of how best to deal with children who have 'ordinary' SEN along with their high ability ('dually exceptional' children). Any approach will benefit from team-work, training and a committed work force. The emotional effects on teachers of shifting control for learning to pupils must be acknowledged, and teachers should be given strategies to help cope with this unusual issue. Also, it must be emphasised that for any initiative to have lasting impact the provision should become 'an integral part of the curriculum, not an add-on' (Goodhew, 2002: 26).

Thinking skills programmes can be incorporated as part of an enrichment strategy or they can be an element of extension or acceleration, depending on the structure and curricula of the school. Some critical thinking skills programmes are presented as strategies for raising standards throughout the school with a variety of ages and abilities and often with a focus on helping the highly able. This seems to fit with the suggestions in the literature and so the efficacy of this approach is now considered.

References

1   The well-publicised case of Ruth Lawrence is perhaps the first and most famous of these cases in the UK, which seem to have become increasingly common. Lawrence, a gifted mathematician, famously won a place at Oxford University in 1981, at the age of ten. Her father accompanied her to university, attending lectures and looking out for her welfare. The media would periodically discuss the pros and cons of her situation, in particular her relationship with her father, by turns the object of scorn and admiration. It is difficult to find data on these cases and unclear whether the incidence is increasing, decreasing or constant. Her experience and that of other child prodigies was reviewed in a BBC4 documentary (January 2004) in which all

the former prodigies expressed dissatisfaction with their schooling experience, largely for reasons of boredom.

2 Initial information from personal communication with the National Association of Gifted Children, July 2001, reinforced by journals.

3 Reference here is to a *Channel 4 Cutting Edge* television documentary March 2003 and a spate of newspaper articles in tabloids and broadsheets.

4 A radical restructure of schools using learning networks was proposed by Illich in his 1971 seminal publication, *Deschooling Society*. Some aspects of his vision for education would complement the ideas of this thesis.

5 This statement was issued in 1994, building on the foundations of the 1989 UN Convention of the Rights of the Child, intending both to improve understanding of children's individual rights within education and welfare. 'The Salamanca Statement was arguably the most significant international document that has ever appeared in the special needs field' stating that '... regular schools with an inclusive orientation are 'the most effective means of combating discriminatory attitudes, building an inclusive society and achieving education for all' (Garner, 1999:52, citing Ainscow, 1997:182).

6 This research was funded by the Economic and Social Research Council and submitted in part completion of a Master of Philosophy degree at Cambridge University in 1990. Two classes of eight-year-olds (total of 74 children) took part in the study, along with their teachers.

7 Gallagher identifies 'sophistication' and 'novelty' as valuable for the able child, in terms of differentiated tasks (2000:689).

8 Baldwin, Vialle and Clarke (2000:570) report the following characteristics: 'Innovation' – teacher is looking for and trying new or different ways to approach learning...focusing her creativity on helping students develop creativity and to become actively involved in learning. 'Gestalt' – well organised with a drive toward completing tasks even at a perfectionist level. This teacher works from where the student is. 'Rapport drive' – sees him or herself as a warm friendly person who students like, works purposefully to build a positive working relationship with the students, which the teacher perceived as beneficial for the students.

7

Critical Thinking Skills Programmes

A child with learning problems: Billie, age 8, Year 4

With learning and organisational problems, Billie was not working to her potential. Her mother was an older single parent, over anxious and desperate to do the right thing for her only child. Once she was identified by a private psychologist as having both dyslexia and dyspraxia, the school set about planning provision to help Billie cope.

The psychologist had used the standard Weschler test (WISC-R) to measure IQ and found an erratic 'spiky score'. This type of test result is typical of able underachievers, but was unfamiliar to the school's special needs teachers, as they had mainly worked with pupils who had these problems with a more regular, low-scoring WISC-R test result. The one-to-one sessions focused on the difficulties and failed to take Billie's high abilities into account. Her reading was excellent, but she was nonetheless required to undertake extra reading, as her weak spelling was wrongly diagnosed as a visual problem, when the problems were to do with her haste to get her many ideas down on paper. No visual problems were recorded on her test score, but the teachers were too busy to create new strategies and tasks.

Billie exhibited low self-esteem and an unusual cluster of difficulties, punctuated by sparks of exceptional understanding and bursts of great ideas. Her particular constellation of characteristics proved too complex for one weekly 40 minute session.

Do you think you're good at learning?

Billie: No. I have ideas, but I don't learn in the right way. My ideas get in the way of the learning because they put me off and I don't do the learning like I have to do it all. I can learn ideas. But not writing ideas.

Critical thinking skills programmes have a focus on the development of reasoning, so they seem especially appropriate as practical provision for the intellectually highly able. But how valuable are such schemes and are they sufficiently grounded in theory and supported by empirical evidence to be recommended?

Because the government supports the inclusion in the National Curriculum of 'teaching thinking', questions are rarely asked about whether this is either achievable or worthwhile. Governmental endorsement is characterised by the key report authored by McGuinness (1999) and for this reason it is a central focus of this chapter, providing the structure for discussion of key issues in the teaching of thinking debate.

A perfect solution for the highly able?

There are several possible reasons why critical thinking skills programmes could be the perfect solution. Firstly, the programmes can be conducted on a stand-alone basis and followed without interfering in usual lesson requirements. Secondly, some materials require little teacher input or monitoring. They are largely designed in a way that would lend them to independent study and sometimes even self-assessment. Lastly and most importantly for the highly able, the programmes are often made up of open-ended tasks. Their flexible structure, adaptability and open-endedness can engage pupils who regularly reach the ceiling in other tasks (Higgins and Baumfield, 1998).

However, contrary to some claims, the programmes cannot be equally applicable to all abilities.[1] Also, programmes are of variable quality and it is difficult for teachers to assess their efficacy. For the programmes to be successful, practitioners will need training to understand the materials and process of the programmes, even when they are used independently by pupils. Lack of confidence in imaginative pedagogy coupled with an over-stuffed National Curriculum has led teachers to seek out a new way to provide challenge whilst not interfering with required subject teaching. Teachers want pupils to become effective learners and can turn to thinking skills programmes to meet this need, particularly when the focus is on challenge for more able pupils. Some create their own schemes, but this practitioner-led research is difficult to maintain and disseminate without substantial funding.[2]

So thinking skills programmes have been well received by teachers partly because they make use of pedagogy teachers would choose anyway, were they not so weighed down by National Curriculum requirements.

> The enthusiasm for thinking skills as a solution to our difficulties with the curriculum stems partly from concern that what is offered in schools today fails to keep up with the current ideas about effective work practice, leisure pursuits and the desire for good-quality relationships. *Haynes, 2002:39*

In addition to their concerns that the current curriculum falls short in meeting the needs of pupils, teachers can be frustrated by an emphasis on quantifiable targets and the associated raised status of curriculum subjects perceived as objectively measurable. Practitioners know that some aspects of learning are not manifested immediately as visible outcomes. The nature of thinking makes it difficult and inappropriate to measure with standard methods. This naturally lowers its status in the eyes of those who champion the drive for ticking boxes in checklists.[3] Philosophy for Children is a critical thinking programme in which this issue is apparent:

> Some of the most important benefits of philosophy will not be quantifiable. During discussion there occur those magic moments whose value is beyond measure. How can you quantify that moment when a very articulate child sitting in the corner of the classroom thinking and not communicating very much suddenly has an idea and is able for the first time to articulate a very thoughtful contribution to a discussion? *Fisher, 1998:245*

'From Thinking Skills to Thinking Classrooms'

Teachers look to academic research and the government to maintain the quality of programmes that make their way onto the market. But what do academics and policy-makers say about these programmes?

Advice is available on the DfES website, often the first resource accessed by teachers, where they can see the government's outline and interpretation of thinking skills. Users would rightly expect the site to present a careful exposition of the area, a wide-ranging and comprehensive taxonomy of skills supported by a rationale for the choices made. This is not what they find. The DfES website notes:

> The National Curriculum states that by using thinking skills, pupils can focus on 'knowing how' as well as 'knowing what' – learning how to learn. The following thinking skills complement the key skills and are embedded in the National Curriculum:
> Information-processing skills/Reasoning skills/
> Enquiry skills/ Creative thinking skills/Evaluation skills.
> *downloaded May 2002*

Nowhere on the website is there any explanation about how such a list was determined. When the ideas are further broken down into what is obscurely termed a 'metadata system', there seems to be a leaning towards certain curriculum subjects. Here, for example, is the set of sub-skills for Enquiry:

> Asking questions/defining problems/questions for enquiry/ choosing equipment/tools/planning research/predicting outcomes/consequences/carrying out research/drawing conclusions/testing conclusions/evaluating process/improving ideas.

There is no suggestion of philosophical enquiry, nor of co-operative work. There is no focus on listening and no mention of time for reflection and contemplation, implying that 'enquiry' is perhaps best suited to scientific, geographical or other empirical subject areas. Clearly, the National Curriculum cannot cover every type of thinking, but the website could at least nod in acknowledgment of the inevitability of gaps in the list. It would be acceptable to assert that what is being presented is not a definitive taxonomy but the comprehensive result of careful choices made for the curriculum by qualified researchers and practitioners in a complex and controversial area. (Scepticism is to be found in the philosophical literature, which continues to worry away at the conceptions so often taken for granted by broader educational literature.[4])

Perhaps it would be more fruitful to seek advice from a pertinent government report published before thinking skills were included in the National Curriculum. This leads us to Carol McGuinness' influential review of thinking skills programmes commissioned by the DfEE in 1998 (published in 1999) and described as 'excellent' by the School Standards Minister.[5] The report concludes that thinking is made up of a range of skills that can be taught, and that these are generalisable and therefore transferable. This leads McGuinness to recommend the teaching of thinking skills in schools, with a particular emphasis on the 'infusion' method, which is the one she adopts for her own classroom materials.[6]

Unfortunately, the report seems like a wasted opportunity to confront the tricky questions plaguing thinking skills. Thorough exposition and analysis built on sturdy foundations with rigorous analysis of empirical and theoretical evidence could have produced a balanced proposal, with thinking skills presented as a useful addition to the classroom teacher's pedagogic toolkit, rather than a universal solution.

Even a cursory glance at the report reveals some irritating errors that hint at a lack of rigour.[7] More seriously, the report lacks critical analysis of basic premises and underpinning theory, somewhat undermining McGuinness' authority. There is no real discussion of the nature of thinking, the importance of subject knowledge is rejected and clarity is lacking about whether the nature of thinking is an attitude, a disposition, a strategy or a mental ability. And there is no attempt to tackle even the well-known criticisms by John McPeck of the concept of thinking skills (1981).

First in a list of five aims, McGuinness asserts that one of the purposes of the review is to '...analyse what is currently understood by the term 'thinking skills' and their role in the learning process' (para 1, p3).

The other four aims focus on practical applications and it is not clear that any of them are thoroughly accomplished in the report. The programmes it examines suppose the existence of thinking skills without question (for example, Sternberg, 1984, and authors of practical resources such as Fisher, 1997; Cam, 1995; Lipman, 1988 and Adey and Shayer, 1994). Without any foundation, McGuinness alleges:

...the idea of thinking-as-a-skill continues to have both theoretical and instructional force. Firstly, it places thinking firmly on the side of 'knowing how' rather than 'knowing that' in the long standing philosophical debate about the nature of knowing. And secondly, much of what we know about skill learning can be usefully applied to developing thinking – being explicit about components of the skills, learning by observation and modelling, the importance of practice, feedback and transfer of learning. *para 2, p4-5*

The presentation of these complex ideas needs more attention if the report is to be robustly defended from critics (Andrews, 1990; Haroutunian-Gordon, 1998; Bailin *et al*, 1999; Baumfield and Higgins, 2001; Bailin and Siegel, 2003). No evidence is presented to prove that thinking is more to do with 'knowing how' than 'knowing that' – an argument that seems to diminish the importance of knowledge. It is possible that some aspects of thinking can be broken down into smaller sub-skills, but this is a contested idea that the report treats as uncontroversial. Whether thinking can be learnt through observation and modelling is also unclear and it is by no means certain that there is transfer of learning across disparate 'thinking skills'. All of these ideas are certainly possibilities, but none are presented within a convincing or thorough framework of argument. They are all underlying suppositions (Johnson and Gardner, 1999; Johnson, 2001).

The focus of the present book is to find provision for the highly able and so the next chapter considers a programme I have found useful for working with the able: Philosophy with Children. This is one of several programmes designed to teaching thinking skills and the remainder of this chapter contextualises them. The programmes fall into three main categories: general; subject specific; and infusion (all quotations in the next three paragraphs are taken from McGuinness, 1999:7).

a) The general approach

Programmes under the 'general' heading use either context-free or context dependent techniques, but are always based on specifically designed materials. They are based on a concept of cognition as 'driven by a general central processor' and aim to intervene and ameliorate thinking through developing this processor.

b) Subject specific

The second method, 'subject specific', considers good thinking to be best developed through specific subject areas and is 'based on the view that high quality thinking is inextricably linked with the knowledge structures, the methods of enquiry and ways of thinking associated with different disciplines or domains.'

c) Infusion

The third way of thinking about thinking is the 'infusion method', in which opportunities for developing different skills are identified through the existing curriculum. Every subject would be used as a vehicle for teaching thinking skills. The National Curriculum would be a curriculum for thinking and lessons would be developed 'where thinking skills and topic understanding are explicitly and simultaneously pursued'.

These three categories are none too clear and some programmes seem to overlap. For example, Cognitive Acceleration through Science Education (CASE) appears to fall into both (a) and (b), aiming to affect cognitive development (a), through concepts taught in science (b). In the report, Philosophy for Children is categorised as a 'general' programme (a), although it does not intend to achieve the cognitive changes central to Feuerstein's Instrumental Enrichment (FIE) or de Bono's Cognitive Research Trust (CoRT), both of them clearly 'general' programmes. Lipman emphasises the development of habits of thinking (Fisher, 1990:156) rather than the 'structural changes' emphasised in FIE (cited in Coles and Robinson, 1989:87). Nowhere does McGuinness mention the development of habits in terms of the general approach. Philosophy for Children could be considered a subject-based or an infusion programme, depending on its interpretation and realisation.

The following sections outline programmes in each category and briefly review underpinning theory, bearing the needs of the able in mind.

The general approach: 'Feuerstein's Instrumental Enrichment' (FIE) and the 'Cognitive Research Trust' (CoRT)

FIE was designed primarily for children with severe learning difficulties, including retarded performers deemed unteachable by mainstream schooling, and is focused on structural cognitive modifiability (Head, 1999). The programme is based on the premise that 'the cognitive structure of the brain can be changed by enabling people to learn how to learn' (Coles and Robinson, 1989:87) and 'more than 100 studies' confirm claims for its efficacy (p92). Amongst students and teachers it has been 'generally well received' (Maclure and Davies, 1991:46).

It presents as well grounded in Vygotskian and Brunerian theory, as well as Feuerstein's own views and it is clearly constructed. The materials have been adapted for wider use, including by the highly able (Blagg *et al*, 1988 'Somerset Thinking Skills Course'). The open-ended nature of the tasks makes them appealing to teachers looking for activities with high ceilings for able pupils, but I have yet to see any specific data on FIE or STSC and the highly able.[8]

FIE does not make use of subject knowledge, not because Feuerstein thinks it irrelevant but because he considers that his target children need initially to master some basic strategies to help them think. De Bono, however deliberately eschews subject learning.[9] His Cognitive Research Trust (CoRT, 1973) is a 'context-free' programme, mentioned in McGuinness' report (although inexplicably not examined but merely listed on page 7). This programme has become a lucrative global business through its apparent applicability to a wide general audience of business and corporate clients as well as educational establishments, and the high sales for his novelty books.[10]

The programme consists of a series of strategies designed to develop a toolkit of skills for use in problem solving and investigative tasks. Tools can be easily taught to children or adults and sessions are diverting and enjoyable, based around tasks such as weighing up 'Plus, Minus and Interesting' aspects of fictional thought-games such as 'What if all cars were yellow?' or 'What if everyone wore a badge to indicate their mood?', a task called 'PMI'. The theoretical underpinning of the CoRT programme is shaky, however, and there is little empirical support for de Bono's claims. Positive claims made by Edwards, for example, lack the appropriate rigour in examining the research tools used to evaluate the outcomes.[11] De Bono seems confused about his own concept of thinking, using muddled metaphors:

> Intelligence is like the horsepower of a car. Thinking is like the skill of the car driver. (1995:iii)

> Thinking is defined as the operating skill with which intelligence acts upon experience. (1992:iv)

> ...thinking will be regarded as a kind of internal vision which we direct at experience in order to explore, understand and enlarge it. It is the deliberate exploration of experience for a purpose. (1976:32)

> The brain is like a car engine. (1970:vi)

> What happens in the brain is information. And the way it happens is thinking. (1969:18)

An obvious criticism of CoRT concerns the lack of evidence for automatic application of the thinking tools in different contexts; it is insufficient merely to assume that building a repertoire of sub-skills will lead to better thinking. Although de Bono argues that following CoRT rigorously will result in this transfer, no supporting evidence exists. There is little provision for learning how to apply the skills to real problems and no substantiation either of how the activities benefit the able, although the website claims that CoRT can be used successfully by 'any age ... any type of thinker' (2000: from website), despite lacking differentiation within the tasks. In earlier writing he is quite rigid about the pace and length of sessions (1976), and it is unclear how this would take account of a range of abilities. I have found the materials quite useful with groups of children of similar abilities, less so in mixed groups.

McPeck finds de Bono's work unexamined by academics, which is surprising given the nature of his claims, but at the same time unsurprising given the non-academic nature of his writings (unsubstantiated claims, no references, rejection of 'the verbal tradition in education', etc., from various references, including 1976: 97.) McPeck notes the 'curious mix of explication and rhetorical persuasion that de Bono uses to promote his ideas' (1981:120), and finds much to criticise in de Bono's mind models, some of which I have noted above.

> There are simply too many types of thinking, manifest in diverse skills, to permit us to infer a single generalised ability for their respective achievement. This is not to deny the inherent merit or usefulness of de Bono's educational prescriptions but merely to point out that his model of the mind is at cross purposes with his prescriptions and cannot serve as a foundation for them. *McPeck, 1976: p104*

Ultimately, McPeck suggests that the methods only really foster the development of divergent thinking and creativity, rather than 'thinking' (p105).

The subject specific approach: Cognitive Acceleration through Science Education (CASE)

This method seems to have impressed the government, with widely reported success as demonstrated by the CASE project (Adey and Shayer, 1989), in which children's cognitive development is accelerated through specific methods of teaching secondary school Science. CASE was originally intended to help pupils with average or below average ability, but has since been taken up by a range of schools. In a recent claim for its success Shayer stated that where there is 'a relatively able intake, schools might expect that between 70 and 80 per cent of their students would achieve grades A-C at GCSE' (*Times Educational Supplement* 23 Feb 2001). Similar programmes in Geography (Leat, 1998 'Thinking Through Geography' cited in McGuinness, 1999) have been established independently, but CASE and allied programmes dominate the subject specific field.[12]

Authors Adey and Shayer have undertaken empirical studies of the effectiveness of CASE and unsurprisingly they have found the programme valuable. The McGuinness Report describes CASE as 'one of the most successful and well-evaluated programmes' (Para 6.2:17) and cites the authors' self-recommendation as evidence for its adoption.[13]

CASE is based on 'pillars of cognitive acceleration' (originally three pillars, now six, Adey and Shayer, 2001:40), and the materials are designed to accelerate the process of moving through Piaget's stages of cognitive development, from concrete to formal operations. This is considered to be natural maturational process that can be speeded up through directed tasks. There are problems with the underpinning stage theory (briefly considered later), but even if this is accepted, it seems that the aims of CASE are unlikely to help the able child. The premise of the programme is that children can be cognitively accelerated and that the highest level to attain is formal operation thought. Able children are already functioning at this higher level if they are in advance of their peers. There is an emphasis on meta-cognition though, which could be helpful to able children in general (Hannah and Shore, 1995; Freeman, 2000; Williams, 2003), and more specifically able underachievers, whose performance-ability gap is marked.

Adey and Shayer accept a notion of general intelligence but do not mind how it is framed or defended.

> Whether we model the underlying general intellectual function in terms of IQ, working memory capacity or on Piaget's *structures d'ensemble* is a matter of fine-tuning. (2001:3)

> ...the process in which people are engaged when they are able to solve a difficult of challenging problem and which results in an improvement in a person's intellectual power. (p36)

> ...empirical data supports the hypothesis of a general cognitive processor which can be positively influenced by appropriate intervention strategies. (p103)

Obviously CASE uses Science, and CAME Mathematics, but exactly how important is subject matter in developing the cognitive powers described above? Adey and Shayer value subject knowledge but 'reject the notion that science might claim a unique position for the development of thinking skills' (1994:79). This, coupled with the proliferation of programmes in other subject areas, demonstrates the importance of subject knowledge and raises questions about the validity of any assumption that thinking skills can be generalised. In earlier editions of CASE, generalising skills explicitly across subjects was not a priority as evidence for general acceleration was considered sufficient (1994:91). The 2001 version, however, incorporates 'bridging' (a term used by Feuerstein in the 1980s) as a 'pillar of cognitive acceleration'.

In general, the efficacy of cognitive acceleration programmes seems to lie in the motivation and increased interest resulting from innovative pedagogy. This implies that teachers will review their teaching methods and start encouraging children to talk about areas of misunderstanding and specific matching of tasks to abilities. For the more able pupil, advanced tasks within the subject area are useful, although probably no more effective than well executed differentiation (See also Bonnett, 1995).

Infusion

Infusion 'exploits naturally occurring opportunities for developing thinking within the ordinary curriculum' (McGuinness, *op cit*:para 7, p19) and is the method underlying McGuinness' own programme, Activating Children's Thinking Skills, (ACTS, 1997).[14] With infusion, every subject area is used as a vehicle for teaching thinking skills, as recognised on the National Curriculum website. At the time of writing (2003) there is still a message promising 'From May 2001, you will be able to use National Curriculum online to search for opportunities to promote thinking skills'. There is also material promoting the ACTS programme.

The ACTS programme was undertaken with seventeen teachers and research findings are based on a review of their experience of 'experimenting in their own classrooms' over an eight month period and after two days of training (McGuinness, *op cit*:para 7.1, p20). No indication is given about the level of ability targeted by ACTS, but one of the findings is that 'children expected to be pushed more' (*ibid*). This benefit was identified through teachers' evaluations, although 'children's learning gains were not monitored' (*ibid*). Other findings are presented without explanation of the terms used. The researchers (the author *et al*) note that:

> Content instruction is invigorated thus leading to deeper understanding; teaching for thoughtfulness is supported across the curriculum; transfer of learning can be more easily promoted and reinforced at other stages. *p19*

Anecdotal evidence is presented to substantiate these conclusions and teachers' comments are quoted to verify the findings, but there is little clarification of underlying ideas, but simply phrases such as 'teaching for thoughtfulness'. I do not doubt the teachers' views, but I find this data insufficient to warrant the promotion of the programme by the government. This is particularly curious when recommendations are not made for other programmes that have equally valid teacher testimony and more compelling empirical evidence.

If this method is indeed effective, the advantages are clear (Quinn, V., 1994). All that is required is a shift in pedagogy and minor adaptation of methods and materials, rather than a radical rethink of the curriculum. These changes can be accomplished by teachers, although time and resources for training must be allocated, and attention paid to the effects of radical pedagogical changes. This may include some kind of modification of power, towards the teacher as facilitator and co-enquirer. McGuinness recognises this, noting that:

> ... classrooms need to have an open-minded attitude about the nature of knowledge and thinking and to create an educational atmosphere where talking about thinking – questioning, predicting, contradicting, doubting – is not only tolerated but actively pursued. *ibid*:15

She also acknowledges the need for teacher development and attending to the 'ethos of schools as learning communities', although how such guidance and support would be provided is unclear.[15]

As with the other programmes, the key discernible positive factor appears to be the way teachers focus on their pedagogy as a consequence of following recommendations.

New kids on the block

New additions to the catalogue of available programmes were obviously unavailable to McGuinness for review, but they introduce new issues and demonstrate the diversity of methods for teaching thinking. These additions have not yet been subject to empirical examination of their effectiveness, but are advertised at government sponsored conferences[16] and form the subject matter of journal articles in both theoretical and practice-based circles, including web-chat and information for Inset providers. There are at least two that need discussion: the World Class Arena (WCA) and Accelerated Learning/Neurolinguistic Programming (NLP).

WCA is a recent innovation and forms part of the Gifted and Talented strategy, since the materials are ostensibly aimed at the highly able. There is substantial funding from the Qualifications and Curriculum Authority (QCA) and an explicit focus on testing, through the World Class Tests (WCT). So far, around 12,000 children have undertaken tests in mathematics and/or problem solving. The tests are contextualised in a web-based scenario called the World Class Arena (WCA), which provides support for teachers, parents and pupils. The tests are available worldwide (at least in the countries that have joined the scheme). This notion of a global arena for high ability implies that cross-cultural core aspects of giftedness must clearly exist and be measurable, which is a contested notion, although no exploration of this is undertaken in the Arena.

Pupils are entered for the tests by their parents and there is a fee to cover administration. The test must be carried out at a registered centre, usually a school. They are completed on a computer and all practice materials are distributed on CD-ROM. Pupils without access to computers are unable to practice and fully participate at this time. Practice tests, support materials and the test fee are only available to those who can pay, benefiting the affluent able and those with motivated parents or teachers.[17] Whilst the materials are good (if narrow – currently just mathematics and 'problem solving'), the issue of access remains a major problem. Potentially positive aspects of WCT and WCA have yet to take hold significantly, but may yet become as popular as US competitions such as the Olympiad and the Odyssey of the Mind, both of which are recommended for the able (Campbell *et al*, 2000).

NLP is at the opposite end of the thinking skills spectrum. Where WCTs are predominantly about test performance, NLP is about changing the way people approach life; the way they think and act in all domains. It is designed for all abilities, but like some of the other programmes mentioned, the open-ended, somewhat unusual tasks, are attractive to teachers struggling to meet a broad range of needs. Many of the tasks are self-explanatory, requiring minimal teacher supervision and allowing pupil autonomy, satisfying the palette of the curious learner. The tasks can also help with the demands of the underachiever as they tap into unconventional ways of learning, possibly unlocking a suitable technique for a pupil with a learning difficulty. NLP is a cluster of strategies that purport to increase efficiency in thought, problem solving and approach to learning. Strategies include dietary supplements, use of music, motivational methods and paying attention to the physical environment. Concept maps or 'mind maps' for note taking (such as those created by Buzan[18]) are also employed, and memory hooks and games can improve memory competence and promote good organisation of ideas and activities.

Some able children find that the techniques free them to work in ways they find more appropriate to their 'thinking style', but this can cause difficulties when they need to re-adapt to school learning. Able underachievers benefit from what amount to study skills strategies and have reported that sessions are less patronising than school-based SEN, which makes the children more likely to attend with a positive attitude.

The WCT and WCA do have on-going research by independent consultants, as the QCA is undertaking continuous evaluation of their efficacy (Waldren, 2003). This is appropriate since they are providing funding. NLP is more of a 'movement' that has its roots in business efficiency ideas and has spread branches into the educational world. Techniques are harnessed by SEN teachers who often embrace methods employing pictures and colour that help students who have learning difficulties or unusual approaches to work due, for example, to their dyslexia and/or Asperger's Syndrome. Neither of these newer programmes has yet engaged formally with debates about issues such as transferability. If they are to be recommended this needs to be taken up.

The impact on teachers

The most valuable changes that thinking skills programmes seem to effect concern pedagogy. The following comments about FIE are typical for a range of programmes:

> The children were consciously thinking problems through ... the teacher wondered whether working with the materials had alerted her to the nature of the problems and changed the way she worked. *Maclure and Davies, 1991:46*

Blagg's findings also emphasised improved teacher skills above anything else (1989), a contention supported by Fisher (1990: 154). Sharron shows the direct link between this and teachers supporting children of different abilities:

> Traditionally they have catered for the middle ability corps and allowed those with learning difficulties and high abilities to cope under inexpertly defined and managed 'differentiated' regimes. *2001:37*

ACTS and CASE research findings echo these notions and McGuinness recognises that the success of these programmes is 'due in no small measure to the well developed teacher training and support' (*op cit*:para 9, p27). Overall, it is clear that the programmes help teachers reconsider their classroom performance and think carefully about how children learn. Subsequent pedagogical changes have far-reaching consequences and it may be that this is the key positive factor of the programmes, regardless of method, aims or structure.

Conclusion

Thinking skills programmes have become increasingly important on the national and international scene and methods, aims and underpinning theories need close examination. For the able, they hold more promise than they deliver. Aspects such as an emphasis on the metacognitive and study skills can be of practical value, but these are normally not central aims of the programmes. Most useful is the way teachers adjust their pedagogy to account for the shift in role that accompanies teaching thinking skills and this is not tied to any single programme.

Conceptualising thinking as a skill or range of sub-skills that can be taught individually and divorced from subject matter, is far too simplistic an approach. Some skills form part of what we call 'thinking' and these can indeed be developed and fostered in school. But to work, they must be accompanied by the development of dispositions and taught within the context of appropriate subject knowledge. Some aspects of learning thinking are related across disciplines, and where this is the case, it should be made explicit. The importance of individual contexts should not be underplayed.

Much of the support for thinking skills programmes is driven by passion for a successful pedagogy that may not be replicated by different practitioners or in different situations. There is also lucrative business in designing and selling programmes, but open debate about underpinning issues and quality of research is lacking. Instead, what we get is one programme's fan club versus another's, and the loudest voice generally wins.

References

1   An example of this is the re-release of Edward de Bono's materials from the 1970s and some of Tony Buzan's study skills work from the 1980s, now available for a wider market. Such adaptations differ from, for example, Blagg's adaptation of Feuerstein's work, in which the entire programme is rethought and recast, rather than merely repackaged, which has happened to some of the afore-mentioned materials.

2   Government agendas determine how funds are distributed for research and this does not favour the practitioner. For example, the influential McGuinness Report (1999), notes the vital need for translating research into practice, but makes no mention of a reversed relationship where ideas for research are born out of practice. A similar research/practice divide is developing in Higher Education. Academics who wish to publish in practitioners' journals are encouraged not to do so, focusing instead on peer-reviewed publications that count towards measures used to determine budgets (currently the Research Assessment Exercise). Peer-reviewed journals are mostly read by academics and professionals actively engaged in further study, whilst the less renowned publications typically have a wider audience, if not an audience in closer contact with children and classrooms. Vital new research therefore fails to reach the audiences who most need to engage with fresh ideas. Similarly, academics fail to keep up to date with the needs of practitioners and practice-based research continues to decline in status and value. An interesting new initiative has been introduced by the Gifted and Talented strategy unit at the DfES (2002) that may help to address this issue. Key stage 1 teachers have been funded for research projects with able pupils. A network has been established to allow for dissemination of this work that has been completed to a high standard and overseen by a steering committee co-ordinated by Brunel University. Funding for continuation of the project is uncertain.

3   For an interesting extension of this argument see Best, 2000.

4   Steve Johnson is described as a 'gadfly' in the journal *Teaching Thinking* (Summer 2001) with reference to his article in the previous edition.

5   Press release from 4th May 1999 where it was noted that 'findings will be fed into the NC Review' This report can be read at www.nc.uk.net/learn_

think accessed in April 2001. No data was available as to the number of teachers accessing the site, but in a personal communication I was told that teachers find the report 'very useful when they are choosing which programme would be best for their school' (May 2001).

6   McGuinness opts for the ACTS project (Activating Children's Thinking Skills project, ACTS), whose title seems to imply that thinking skills are somehow innate and dormant, awaiting the stimulation of a planned programme to galvanise them into action.

7   Such as calling Matthew Lipman 'Martin Lipman' (5.4, p13), misinterpreting Murris' work with story books as 'a pictorial version of philosophy' (5.4, p14) and using the disparaging term 'cottage industry' to describe academic research on children's understanding of scientific concepts (6.2, p17).

8   Some critics note that the serialistic and analytical approach could be counter-productive for some careful, able workers. The method is appropriate for those who need support in building these strategies, 'but not good for those pupils who were already over reflective, perfectionist and anxious about making mistakes' (Jones and Jones, 1992:2). High task ceilings make some activities eminently suitable for the able, however.

9   He considers that subject content offers 'comparatively little scope for thinking except of the hindsight variety' (1976:104).

10 For a list of companies and others using his work see his website, at www. edwDeBono.com.

11 Edwards' work (1991) for example, lacks rigour in examining the research tools used to evaluate outcomes of CoRT activities (cited in Maclure and Davies *op cit*).

12 Parallel programmes are run in Mathematics and Technology (CAME, 1998 and CATE, 2001) underway as well as the development of materials for younger children at Key Stage 1 (CASE@KS1, 2001) amongst others. This is partly due to the government funded Centre for the Advancement of Thinking, based at King's College and directed by Phillip Adey, from which research can be undertaken and programmes developed.

13 In their 2001 publication, there is no mention among the eight pages of references of any study evaluating their programme that is not by Adey, Shayer or both (pp196-203). This seems unusual for a well-funded programme running for more than a decade.

14 Whether this can be correctly termed 'infusion' is questioned by Johnson, who points out that 'to infuse' is defined as to 'introduce into one thing a second which gives it extra life, vigour and a new significance' (2001:4). This is not necessarily demonstrated by the ACTS methodology using the existing curriculum.

15 The Schools' Standards Minister announced that training would be available for teachers in the area of thinking skills. 'The government will ensure thinking skills are addressed in the curriculum and in the guidance on teaching. We will give teachers access to appropriate training in the teaching of thinking skills' (E. Morris, 4 May 1999). Such training has yet to be delivered as a coherent national strategy.

16 They are often marketed at the DfES termly Standing Conference and other conferences such as the annual National Association of Able Children in Education (NACE) meeting and the biennial 'Thinking' conference.

17   Developers of materials have suggested that success in the tests could be advantageous in schoolchildren's Curriculum Vitae, now a vital component in the fight for a place in a selective school. This would disadvantage those without access to the test. At the aforementioned thinking skills conference in Harrogate, delegates were split over their views of the WCTs, with some delighted to have found what they had been searching for but just as many teachers hostile to the very idea of testing. Overriding concerns were for how testing can stifle imagination, channelling pupils into yet more Mathematics, while others worried about issues of payment and pressure both on and from parents. In my view, all the old arguments about support for the gifted being a factor in the perpetuation of elitism are fuelled through the development of such texts. (Information gleaned from conference sessions and talking to people on the stand.)

18   Tony Buzan's latest publication is *Mind Maps for Kids* (2003) which takes his concept map ideas from the 1980s and updates them for children. These are popularly used by NLP practitioners, but were not designed for these programmes.

8

Philosophy with Children

A child turned against the system: Eva, age 11, Year 7

Eva found the transition from primary to secondary education difficult. Accustomed to an open, questioning atmosphere, the freedom to control topic work and plan her own tasks, she now had to deal with compartmentalised subjects that were taught fairly rigidly. It is typical of her style of thinking that in one instance she saw a connection between what she had learned in a physics class and a new concept in biology. When she remarked on this, she was reprimanded for 'doing the wrong subject in a biology lesson' and asked to leave class.

As this happened several times in different classes, her classmates were soon competing to time how long it would take before certain teachers sent Eva out of the room for 'impertinence'. Eva's sense of humour endeared her to a range of different friendship groups and she began to treat school as just a place to be with her friends. Teachers were divided about her ability. Some noted her flashes of advanced thinking and interesting ideas whereas others dismissed her as intellectually weak, lazy, and wasting a coveted place at the selective school. Her truanting became a problem.

Do you think you're good at learning?

Eva: I used to be. I was okay at primary, but mainly because I could do my own thing. Everything here is about doing what you are told and not mixing up ideas. In primary we were supposed to mix up

125

ideas, which is what I am good at. They don't want me here and I don't want to be here. It's a waste of time. If you don't say anything they tell you to speak up and if you do, they chuck you out of class. You can't win. There's at least five more years. I wanted to go to University, but if it's just the same as school what's the point?

Of the numerous critical thinking skills programmes, I have chosen to look at Philosophy with Children (P4C/PwC) in detail as it seems the most useful for children of high ability, a view based not only on theory and literature but also on classroom practice. I have adopted the following definitions:

> The abbreviation PwC is used ... to refer to the practitioners of philosophy with children. The term 'P4C' is used as an abbreviation for the proponents of the 'Philosophy for Children' programme developed by Matthew Lipman and colleagues from the Institute for the Advancement of Philosophy for Children (IAPC) in the USA. 'PwC' stands for a larger group of people than 'P4C' because not all children's philosophy teachers believe the IAPC material is the best educational material with which to introduce young children to philosophy. *Murris, 2000: 277*

PwC is often presented alongside Critical Thinking Skills programmes and evaluated using the same criteria. A variety of different programmes and pedagogies fall under the umbrella heading, and since they have been gaining momentum worldwide, Philosophy for/with Children has become known as a 'movement', implying a shared ideology and a sense of organised group action, perhaps imbued with a sense of evangelism. PwC has many supporters, mainly in the USA, UK, Australia and Latin America,[1] but also numerous detractors, whose critiques are presented here.

What is PwC?

The birth of the P4C movement is uncontroversially attributed to Matthew Lipman, who created materials for children and teenagers in order to help them develop the dispositions of reasoning required for later study of philosophy at university level. He established a training centre for teachers (IAPC), and teacher education is a key focus of the programme. Lipman cites Dewey as a major influence on his work, particularly in interpreting education as reasoning, encouraging the 'fostering of thinking', and rejecting a model of teaching that is little more than transmission of knowledge (Lipman, summarised in Whalley, 1987:269). The P4C programme consists of a series of novels and teachers' notes. PwC can include a range of materials with stimuli such as news stories, picture books and art.

Many practitioners are now interested in PwC but have departed from some of Lipman's tenets, creating their own interpretations and materials.[2] Some principles are upheld both by those advocating PwC and those who choose P4C. These principles include the aim of effective moral development, as there is a strong sense that PwC is about making children become better people in general, but this is difficult to evidence through empirical research. Some aspects of learning are impossible to quantify and the focus is usually on what can be measured and tested. Improved literacy and numeracy through PwC have been demonstrated in research, but this was never part of Lipman's original agenda.

Another key feature in all types of PwC/P4C programmes is the 'Community of Enquiry'. This is a democratic discussion in which the children set the agenda and the teacher's role is to facilitate a group enquiry. Children are encouraged to think 'logically, critically and creatively, to reason and reflect, and to deliberate with an open-minded disposition' (Haynes, 2002:12).

Some activities on the fringe of PwC carry with them a sense of evangelism, lacking rigorous examination of key principles and incorporating rather unusual activities. Whilst there is nothing wrong with being unconventional, rationales are needed for all proposals, outlandish or ordinary. But they are seldom provided in PwC. Medical and other evidence suggests that dietary recommendations, meditation and visualisation exercises can be helpful, but to confuse this with an emphasis on critical thinking and reasoning is mistaken. Critics of PwC have an easy target if they want to discredit the requirement to have children seated on bean-bags and drinking a cup of water every 20 minutes. Certainly, paying heed to the learning environment can be helpful, and must be recognised as relevant, but as incidental rather than as the substance of a programme for teaching thinking.

PwC is a global concern, with the UK, USA and Australia as leading countries in the developed world. Countries in South and Central America have embraced PwC (particularly Brazil and Mexico), and less developed European countries are also attracted to the pedagogies because of the underpinning notion of developing autonomous thinkers. In order to create a democracy or to help rebuild a country after a revolution, education must reflect major societal changes, by allowing pupils to learn how to express themselves effectively. And this is where PwC can play an important role.[3]

Claims against the efficacy of PwC come from different sources. Here I consider the more commonly expressed objections, later highlighting particular aspects that concern the highly able.

Objection 1: PwC is no more than standard classroom discussion work

Teachers employ a variety of techniques to encourage discussion in the classroom, such as Circle Time. Philosophy programmes are specific about how their discussion differs from these standard classroom techniques. The key difference is the creation of a 'Community of Enquiry', with specific conventions and guidelines. Techniques overlap with good teaching practice – helping children create their own group rules; sitting in such a way that group members can see one another; talking in turns; respecting other people's views, etc. But with the Community of Enquiry, pupils are also invited to set the agenda. This is less often found in other classroom work, where teachers hold debates designed to emphasise a predetermined teaching point.

In the Community of Enquiry, the teacher provides a stimulus to encourage pupils to think about what they would like to investigate, agreeing on a specific focus. Then, using a democratic process, the group decides what they will investigate, devolving power and choice to the children. Once the enquiry is underway, children are encouraged to make their disagreements the focus of the discussion, in a respectful way. Specific techniques help ease this process and pupils have clear guidelines about being assertive but not aggressive. For example, they might begin each sentence with 'I dis/agree with x because...', making it acceptable to disagree or agree with anyone in the class, whether they are established friends or just classmates.

This is not always the case in class work, where there is often peer pressure to agree with friends. Here though, the group is working together, pursuing a line of enquiry where children are encouraged to say what they really think, even if they hold an unpopular view. Children are allowed to disagree with one another, but have to show logic and reasoning in their thinking and their contribution should be relevant to the group task of striving to find answers to the questions under investigation.

> ...the very notion of 'critical thinking' and the goal of the community of inquiry as that of progression forward in the comprehension of an idea assumes that there is indeed something to be grasped and that it is more or less graspable. When we sketch out the role of the facilitator in the inquiry we explicitly detail qualities of thinking that are desirable and worthy of promoting and those that are not. *Turgeon, 1998:19*

In ordinary Circle Time, the teacher usually encourages pupils to join together, tacitly agreeing that the dominant set of values should be used to create a common moral code. Children are expected to find examples that agree with the teacher's suggestions (why we should share, not drop litter, allow people to join in our games, etc) and pupils are aware that the sessions are about signing up to common ideals, not explaining how they really feel about issues. In PwC, pupils are encouraged to have their own divergent views as long as they are supported with reasoning and argument. Whalley explains:

> It is only by the most careful listening that the teacher will become aware of the range of opinions on a given topic, and be able to devise questions to promote dialogue between the protagonists. ... The teacher does not so much lead a discussion as facilitate its being led by the group. There is more. It is the teacher's job to notice mistakes in the reasoning that are overlooked by the group, and devise ways of drawing attention to them; to insist that those doing the most talking are also prepared to listen, and to make sure that those who prefer to talk less have the opportunity to express themselves when they wish. *Whalley, 1987:270*

The PwC process is certainly different from ordinary classroom discussion work.[4]

Objection 2: children cannot cope with abstraction

This claim assumes philosophy and philosophical problems to have a significant degree of abstraction and that children are unable to engage with this way of thinking. Effective philosophising must involve the ability to hold concepts in mind and manipulate them to build logical argument. Issues under discussion can be framed in more or less accessible ways but they will almost always involve a higher degree of abstraction than the usual tasks undertaken in the classroom.

The notion of children being unable to think abstractly stems from Piaget's influential developmentalist ideas, to which there have been objections.

> In sum, Piaget's theory asserted that there is a single route of intellectual development that all humans follow, regardless of individual differences, although their progression along this route may be at different rates and they may stop off on the way rather than follow the route to completion. Studies contest the invariant sequence of the individual psychological operations within a stage (Dasen, 1977) ... there may be more than one developmental route to the acquisition of some constructs.
>
> Lack of attention to individual differences points to the limited usefulness of the theory in explaining and predicating many aspects of performance. *Sternberg, 1990:180-181 and 190*

The replicability of Piaget's tests has been widely discussed, with well-documented criticisms, in particular the work of Donaldson (1978 and Sutherland, 1992). More fundamental criticisms of developmental theory can be found in the philosophical work of David Hamlyn, John White and Chris Winch. White rehearses the objections to development as unfolding, citing Hamlyn (1992:78-9), and Winch also notes:

> There are two massive problems associated with most developmental theories; the first is that they seek to show what children cannot learn at certain ages. The second is that, rooted squarely in the metaphor of organic growth, they find it difficult to account for motivation. *1998*

Gazzard summarises the usual responses to Piagetian charges as follows:

1. Attempting to find weaknesses in Piaget's theory (Gareth Matthews);

2. Interpreting Piaget in such a way that theory can be made to accommodate the possibility of philosophy for children (Hope J. Haas);

3. Ignoring the discrepancy between practising philosophy for children on the one hand and thinking in Piagetian terms on the other. *1989:11*

She concludes that it is not as much a refutation of Piaget that is needed, but rather a reinterpretation that allows developmentalism to be only one possible explanation. Freeing an understanding of cognitive development from the developmentalist stage theory allows for the view that 'cognitive growth is predominantly a function of learning' (p13).

> ...insofar as children are no longer limited in terms of their cognitive capacities by maturation, there is no reason to suspect that given the appropriate information they might not manifest and be proficient in abstract thinking at young ages. *ibid*

This is certainly a useful framework for thinking about the able child. It generously allows for wide individual difference. But it is not altogether clear how useful it would be to reinterpret Piaget in order to accommodate this way of thinking about cognitive development. Such a rethink would incorporate looser understandings of the ages assigned to stages and an acceptance of a more gradual and messier transition through the stages, for example. I am not sure it is necessary to shoe-horn Gazzard's ideas into a developmentalist framework, but she insists that the Piagetian viewpoint could be 'extended eventually to accommodate this role of education and the consequent viability of philosophy for children' (*op cit*). There is still value, though, in challenging developmentalist understandings of cognitive development.

Many theorists and practitioners agree that Piagetian stage theory underestimates children's ability to abstract ideas (White, 1985; Smutny *et al*, 1997; Tucker and Hafenstein, 1997, Murris, 2001).

Barbara Tizard and Martin Hughes support this, particularly through their careful examination of children's use of language and the quality of their participation in conversation:

> Young children are much less egocentric and illogical than Piaget believed. We found many examples ... of their awareness of, and interest in, other people's viewpoints. By the age of three or four, we would argue that dialogue is as important as physical exploration. *1990:19*

Richard Kitchener, however, argues that children are capable of only 'concrete' not 'abstract' philosophy as they are unable to make inferences about underlying principles, and White wonders if children can really manage higher order thinking. If the developmental theories are abandoned, it would be a case of taking each child on their merits and this may allow for some to be capable of reasoning at high levels at an early age. Even with the developmentalist theory intact, it could be argued that highly able pupils just move through the stages at a greater speed than most children. This being so, they would be capable of abstract thought and thus benefit from undertaking PwC activities in development of this aspect of their learning.

Some children do seem to demonstrate firm abilities in abstract thinking. These issues arise again in Objection 4, as they impact on the concept of 'real philosophy' as involving abstraction.

Objection 3: empirical evidence to support PwC is inadequate

Most of the empirical evidence available considers the efficacy of P4C schemes, as collated by IAPC. Systematically constructed research programmes have not been commonly undertaken in the broader PwC arena and while there is anecdotal evidence and practitioner action research that supports the programmes, little other substantiation can be presented. Existing evidence focuses on general improvements in reading, comprehension and mathematics, not on reasoning. Pupils have not been tested specifically for philosophical understanding or reasoning, either before or after a PwC programme.

Empirical evidence seems only to examine transferability, which is not a key programme aim. Checking improvements in mathematics and English is not a method used to justify the value of other areas of the curriculum, such as history or art. Why must it be assumed that this is relevant for philosophy?

PwC does tend to spring up where a specific practitioner demonstrates enthusiasm for this particular way of working. Whilst not exclusive to PwC, it is certainly symptomatic, resulting in patchy provision where success is doubtless due partly to the commitment of participants and therefore difficult to generalise.

A parallel can be drawn with the development of *Sesame Street*, the hugely successful and popular television show of the late 1960s and 1970s, and still thriving today.[5] The show was established to help compensate for language deficits among poor and immigrant children, who were disadvantaged in starting school. Original claims that the show would help children learn about sharing, caring, harmonious multicultural living and present different racial groups with positive role models had to be played down because of the lack of reliable tests for these wide-ranging goals. What could be examined however, was children's recognition of numbers and letters and their basic conceptual understanding of positional words such as 'above and below', simple processes, like baking and melting, and typical language associated with pre-school curricula, such as the weather, items of clothing, shapes, colours and transport. *Sesame Street* excelled in meeting these concrete objectives, but the research results represent an impoverished notion of the purpose of the programme.

Adults influenced by the programme cite the role models and specifically remember the people from different ethnic groups presented as successful entrepreneurs, and as friends across social and racial divides. In these days of accountability, testing and quantification, more nebulous and complex aspects of interaction and development are difficult to prove. The danger is that things that can't be definitively proved are then discounted as lacking value. PwC and *Sesame Street* have the same problems in this sense, but *Sesame Street* has reached a broader audience. The programme makers have been vindicated in their aims, as anecdotal evidence continues to affirm the success of aims that, though admirable, had been diminished in importance because they could not be definitively tested. It is still unclear, however, how it is possible to check accurately such qualitative learning as moral reasoning.

Perhaps transcripts of dialogues could be used. Kitchener suggests that it would count as evidence, if children:

> ... questioned on a one-to-one basis about their comments [could] elaborate on their views and rationally defend them. 1990:426-7

Murris suggests that this would be more convincing than the 'one time performances or philosophical one-liners' that Kitchener would not accept as evidence, but also notes that this discounts the value of collaborative thinking ('thinking together like one big head') and that the role of the Community of Enquiry is so important in PwC that it should play a part in assessment (2000:264). Quality of anecdotal evidence and reported dialogues must also be assured, if this is to serve as proof of learning.

Another difficulty with empirical evidence in this area is the impossibility of knowing how well the materials have been either taught or learnt. With so few teachers working in the field and some materials relatively untested, there are real possibilities of weak teaching and mistakes arising through misunderstanding of materials, which could then be misrepresented as the children having difficulties with ideas.

There are inherent difficulties with assessing children's progress in philosophy and empirical evidence has concentrated instead on more commonly measured subjects with no direct relation to the programmes being reviewed. Until independent large-scale studies are undertaken and programmes are more widespread and systematic, empirical questions will remain unanswered.

Objection 4: PwC is not real philosophy

It is difficult to provide a single, clear definition of philosophy, as the field covers a range of activities and material. Gazzard is particularly interested in Lipman's work and presents the following three definitions of philosophy which capture some commonly expressed views:

(1) ...philosophy as a type of striving associated with seeking to know how to live a better life;

(2) a view which renders it a specific body of problems and/or the history of the ideas of past and present philosophers;

(3) philosophy as a particular way of thinking most often cast as reflective thinking ... and critical appraisal. *1996:9*

The first conception was a focus of earlier writings of Lipman, but as Gazzard notes:

> ... the relationships between reasons for belief and knowledge is controversial ... the search for meaning is, therefore, not as straightforward as the earlier writings of Lipman and his co-workers suggest. *p15*

Teachers need an appropriate attitude to their work in order to encourage and foster these dispositions.

The second conception of philosophy involves learning about and understanding an important body of work that is generally reserved for degree level work. The accusation of PwC as diluted philosophy is reasonable if this reduced conception is acceptable as a definition. However, PwC is considered as more to do with active participation, the ideas of great philosophers being used as stimulus for developing children's reasoning. Critics such as Kitchener consider that children should do philosophy in the same way as academic philosophers do, although this argument is not used for other curriculum subjects.[6] Murris suggests it could be fair to consider children's progress alongside novice adult philosophers, but not against qualified academics (2000:262-3).

Matthews considers that children should not be assessed according to adult criteria. He views PwC as different from adult philosophy (1978:71-2) and maintains that philosophical questions 'should not be considered the exclusive province of professional philosophers' (1984:3). This is supported by Walter Kohan:

> To impose our creations and our manner of creating them is to impose our experience of the world, and thereby to impede them from reflection on their own experience. *1998:8*

Murris rejects this argument as not going far enough to combat the critics whom she accuses of failing to offer sufficient arguments for their notions of 'real philosophy' (*op cit*:266-7).

With reference to the third of Gazzard's conceptions, PwC meets the criteria for reflective and critical thinking. Again, this is as much to do with inculcating dispositions as introducing new subject knowledge. PwC differs pedagogically from other curriculum subjects. It is 'real philosophy' in that children are encouraged to develop skills and attitudes that help them reason and that the work 'reflects the dialogic character of philosophical thinking' (1996: 276). As there are no definitive answers, the enquiry is genuine, and if teachers use recommended methods, they will facilitate the development of discussion. By being a co-enquirer they help children probe and deepen ideas, not by blindly accepting all contributions but by pointing out errors of logic and lack of reasoning and working with the group to aim for finding the truth.

Objection 5: Children lack the concentration and focus necessary for philosophy and are not sufficiently interested in the research and enquiry needed to pursue philosophical questions

If the task is motivating, children will spend time pursuing relevant information in search of an in-depth answer. Whether this would happen with philosophy is an empirical question, which is currently unanswerable as the subject is not on the curriculum for young children.

Some people will find philosophy intrinsically motivating, but it can be made more accessible in the first instance through carefully planned pedagogy. Lipman aimed to make the experience of P4C 'acceptable and enticing' and this evoked an enthusiastic response. The popularity of sessions is noted in the literature (e.g. Haynes, 2002:58-9; Fisher, 1998:7; Sapere website, etc) and echoed here by Costello:

> [Yet] one of the reasons why the children to whom I have taught philosophy over the years looked forward to our sessions so much is precisely that they enjoyed themselves so much. *2000: 37*

This is likely to increase commitment to completing set tasks and pursuing ideas beyond the classroom, but is it really representative of the process of doing philosophy? White does not think so:

> Philosophy often brings bewilderment, despair, painful struggles for understanding. ... presenting philosophy to children as a fun activity may impede rather than promote any understanding they may come to have of what philosophy is all about.
> *1992:77*

Many school activities are designed to be enjoyable for children and it is hoped that the cognitive dissonance they experience when learning provides the sort of challenge that keeps them interested in exploring ideas and finding out about their world. Any number of things in a school day will cause frustration and upset: completing a painting, climbing a rope, solving an equation, writing a letter. Hard and interesting tasks are often popular with children and their definition of fun may well include a certain amount of struggle. Naturally, we all have different strengths, and the appeal of philosophy may be no more widespread than that of other activities such as chemistry, sprinting or singing in the choir. Teachers do not necessarily worry about whether their laboratories, starting blocks or conducting techniques are a real representation of the professional version of their activity. It is certain that a good many children do enjoy PwC, but whether they have a true sense of 'real philosophy', or professional philosophy, is a question yet to be addressed by research.

Some pupils, particularly the highly able, show a remarkable level of sustained interest. Projects in philosophy certainly can be harder to undertake than in disciplines in which a clear end is more obvious. But this would not disallow highly able pupils from demonstrating their ability and drive to explore difficult questions. They might need a helping hand to ensure that they conduct a useful investigation. When children have a humanities project to complete, for example, they are encouraged to persist in questioning, helped to structure their argument, and directed to gather pertinent information. Children are rarely given this kind of help when they raise philosophical questions because teachers and parents know better how to help pupils with more familiar enquiries. If pupils are not helped to follow through initial interests, we cannot tell whether they would demonstrate commitment and ability in finding, or moving towards, useful and well-considered answers.

Philosophy and highly able children

As well as being popular with ordinarily able pupils, PwC has a great deal to offer highly able children. Indeed, many of the objections are negated.

- Objection 1: PwC differs from classroom work, is an empirical issue

- Objection 2: children's ability to think abstractly is a defining features of many definitions of high ability

- Objection 3: there needs to be more empirical evidence

- Objection 4: whether or not PwC constitutes 'real philosophy' depends on pedagogies, materials and systems

- Objection 5: concerns about children's intellectual stamina are irrelevant to the highly able.

Key features of PwC make it suitable for the highly able.

a) There are no ceilings or limits

As there are no absolute answers in philosophical enquiry, the depth of enquiry depends on the abilities of the children. The common cry that 'I've finished already' does not apply. The questions and ideas under investigation are involved and complex, allowing children to develop a better sense of how to follow through an in-depth, challenging enquiry.

A discussion of war with six able nine-year-olds is a typical illustration of this. Having read a newspaper article brought in by a pupil, we considered some of the issues it raised, as a Community of Enquiry. The children decided on the central question 'Should you care about war if it doesn't touch your life?' and proceeded to debate and argue, backing up their ideas with reason and challenging one another. During the week, half the group sought me out to show me some extra unbidden work they had started (a concept map on 'war in school' considering what war meant to them in terms of daily friendship battles, playground turf wars and arguments with teachers). The informal, out-of-class project lasted for a whole term, with the three girls researching and discussing, writing and presenting ideas informally. They said that it was an exciting project because there was no end and they could keep going forever. They were clearly motivated and enjoying the work.

b) PwC provides opportunities to explore abstract ideas

PwC allows the able to explore complex notions, engaging them in ideas that they may have been discouraged from considering due to the constraints of the curriculum, which compels teachers to steer away from issues that do not match set targets. However, abstract ideas often tap into particular interests of the highly able, such as questions about the nature of life and death and the existence of God.

Even younger able pupils seem interested in questions that are not easily answered through empirical evidence. I have witnessed and facilitated many Communities of Enquiry where children tackle abstract ideas and respond with good answers that demonstrate their appreciation of the complexities of the topics. I have met children interested, for example, in ideas of infinity and the mind-body issue. Merely raising questions such as 'If I have a soul, where is it?' or 'What's the most important thing in the entire world?' may not indicate abstract understanding, but following it up and investigating the idea demonstrates something more substantial. The soul question was raised by Stan, and our discussions on the topic lasted the whole year we were together in school. They took place mainly when I was on playground duty, and we followed up research he undertook unbidden in his own time. He started his investigations with the etymology of the word and found a range of meanings for 'soul' and 'sole'. He was particularly interested in the different spellings for '*sole*, a part of the body you can see, and *soul*, a part of you that you can't see'. Looking carefully at language and its use is a common starting point for philosophical investigations of some concepts and Stan had come to this through his own interests. With encouragement he went on to explore related uses of words such as 'soulful' and 'soul music', and then found himself in the realms of 'spirituality and the soul'. Through reading and discussing he demonstrated an extended investigation of an abstract issue.

c) PwC is particularly useful for underachieving able pupils

As it does not have to involve writing, PWC can be an excellent opportunity for children with learning difficulties to express their ability. Success in PWC sessions does not depend upon the usual factors at which these pupils so often fail. Creating a Community of Enquiry is a different pedagogy from customary teaching approaches and can prove appealing for pupils who are finding ordinary classes frustrating. Success positively affects self-esteem and this can have a good all-round impact.

One underachieving pupil, Dave, was nervous of admitting his unusual ideas in class. He would always preface his stranger contributions with 'I heard on the radio...' or 'I read in a Sunday magazine...' to avoid being teased. He confessed that the ideas were his own, but that he was embarrassed to express them because he had been laughed at for their outlandish nature. In the PwC sessions, Dave's weirder ideas were embraced and he began to take credit for his own thoughts in ordinary class sessions, qualifying them with statements such as 'You might think I'm making a silly comment, but hear the whole thing first. I can explain how I thought of it.'

It is through discussion that many children show the flashes of ability that eventually lead to their identification as highly able. Children have positively looked forward to sessions. Enthusiasm for school learning was untypical among the children featured at the start of each chapter, except for André and Doris, and teachers remarked on the positive effect of sessions on all the pupils' ordinary classwork. Recommendations for the underachieving able made by key writers (Freeman, Montgomery, Wallace) match well with the pedagogy of PwC. These include aspects such as metacognitive work, an emphasis on unusual ideas, open-ended tasks and engaging with difficult notions.

Billie and Charlie particularly benefited from being able to express their ideas in discussion without the ubiquitous 'write it all up' requirement characteristic of many school tasks. One underachieving able pupil was a talented cartoonist and took to recording some aspects of the discussion in cartoon form. His humour and understanding were clearly visible in the work, which he produced in his own time, without prompting. His teacher was amazed at the sophistication of his drawing and his ideas, which were far more impressive than ever indicated in his typically below average written work.

d) PwC challenges pupils who already achieve highly

For these children PwC is useful in two ways. It provides challenge for children who are in danger of being bored by easy tasks, and it compels teachers and able achievers to rethink their understanding of successful responses to set tasks. Philosophy challenges the 'one right answer' culture of high-achievers and allows different pupils to excel. The complacent able pupil can be unsettled by the achievement of others around them, and by the challenge of having to adapt the way they respond to tasks.

> Interestingly, the few dissenting voices often come from those children who are clever in the traditional academic sense. They are puzzled and resentful when they realise that philosophical questions are not amenable to simple, straightforward answers – even from the teacher! Such children have unfortunately been trained to perceive educational value only in what can be examined and tested. *Whalley, 1987:73*

The aim is not to perturb pupils, but it is surely better to experience such confusion while still at school, in an environment in which anxieties can be expressed and tackled. Knowing that learning and understanding is about more than merely uncovering a predetermined correct answer is a useful lesson, one more closely related to 'real life' scenarios.

Presenting a PwC 'picture books session' is of particular interest in this case, as high achievers regard it as far too easy when they are introduced to the session. As the community takes off, they begin to see the potential depth of the activity and are drawn into the discussion. The most puzzled looks and furrowed brows are often on the faces of the able high achievers. I have even seen anger from such children because they felt threatened by the freer form of sessions. With practice and experience, however, they began to participate more readily and all the children who initially expressed dislike eventually grew to enjoy the work.

e) PwC is flexible

Practical aspects of PwC allow for its inclusion into the school day with reasonable ease. It can be taught in or out of class, as specific sessions for the able, or with a mixed ability group. Providing extension work for the more adept is simple and need not affect the school curriculum, being run, for example, as clubs or extra classes. As it can make use of a range of stimuli, PwC can be taught virtually without materials or resources.

Sessions always reflect the children's interests and can be adapted by them to take into account issues of the day, be they international news items or local, school and personal issues. As a Senco, I have had to teach many last minute, fill-in sessions, or run sessions with far fewer or far more pupils than originally anticipated and I find that philosophy can be easily adapted for such situations.

Conclusion

I remain uncomfortable with the concept of P4C/PwC as a 'movement' and feel that the proponents of P4C and PwC will have to take criticisms more seriously if they are to have their ideas accepted in the mainstream. From the early work of Lipman to the current available activities there have been significant changes, some of which would definitely count as improvements, but the lack of empirical research is holding back further development. As with any good programme, some aspects are excellent, but some reasonable reservations remain.

PwC is a possible practical contribution to dealing with the highly able. It can enrich the curriculum, or provide extra, out-of-school provision and it could allow pupils to remain in mixed classes and yet be challenged and encouraged through stimulating activities.

References

1   'In Brazil alone more than 30,000 children are involved in P4C programmes that are helping to raise the standards of literacy' (Fisher, 2003:33).

2   The Society for the Advancement of Philosophical Enquiry and Reflection in Education (Sapere) was established by Roger Sutcliffe and Steve Williams and is the largest PwC organisation in the UK; Karin Murris authored 'Storywise' using picture books; Antidote (the national organisation for Emotional Literacy) advocate PwC; Robert Fisher writes teacher-friendly books with accessible PwC ideas; LEAs such as Northumberland have a strong network of PwC teachers and specialists; the International Council of Philosophic

Inquiry with Children (ICPIC) has members worldwide; Philip Cam in Australia and numerous organisations in Latin America and Eastern European countries in particular.

3   The organisation IAHE (International Association for the Humanisation of Education) is an example of this. Members are committed to helping post-communist countries use education to build democracy.

4   For a thorough explanation of the difference between Circle Time and creating a Community of Enquiry, see Haynes, 2002 and Fisher, 1998.

5   Produced by the *Children's Television Workshop*.

6   As with other academic subjects, this does not mean that teachers should not have appropriate backgrounds. The IAPC materials and SAPERE courses require some specific study of philosophy for teachers.

Conclusion

The children

It would be good to report that the children featured in this book all went on to resounding success once their high ability and, in some cases, difficulties had been identified. Unfortunately, this is not the case. Most of the children have had a patchy few years with a mixed bag of happy and unhappy experiences. I hope the government strategy will help to equalise the quality of provision for children such as these, or at least raise their profile. It seems that in many schools, teachers are reluctantly taking on the role of co-ordinating the programme for the able, often without the training, support or time to give the children what they are entitled to and what they need.

In many places, though, the picture is less bleak. Enthusiastic practitioners are discovering the rich rewards that come from engaging in challenging work with able pupils. I hope this book helps teachers, parents and policy makers in their arguments for supporting the able pupil.

Able children are an anomaly. They do not fit traditional models of ability and intelligence and they do not fit standard educational provision in schools. Being clear about what is meant by high ability is difficult. Deciding what resources they require and the level of support they are entitled to receive is also complex, partly because this involves separating the political from the educational. The research field 'is more or less fragmented, with results that cannot be easily compared to one another' (Ziegler and Raul, 2000).

This interdisciplinary book contributes to the debate about what it is fair to do for able children. Using psychological perspectives as well as considering aspects of practice and analysis of underpinning premises from a philosophical angle has enabled me to clarify common but rarely examined ideas and connect theory and research to practice.

Implications for research

As this is an interdisciplinary book, it raises particularly wide issues that merit research and investigation. These emanate from each of my three key themes. For example, questions concerning the nature of high ability and intelligence merit pursuing, as well as empirical work into the efficacy of PwC and further conceptual work on the notions underpinning thinking skills. In my view, the key area for research is how to ensure challenge for the able.

Understanding and defining challenge is complex, as it necessarily has to take personal interests and abilities into account. A review of different conceptions of challenge may well reveal some common factors though, and it would not be surprising if these relate to Vygotsky's Zone of Proximal Development (ZPD) and Piagetian understandings of cognitive dissonance. Traditionally, these ideas are presented as differing considerably in terms of the role of interaction between novice and experienced learners. Cognitive dissonance is often described in terms of task-setting for individuals (or less often, groups), while ZPD tasks relate more to the development of independent abilities that currently need the scaffolding of an experienced peer or adult. This immediately provides both activities to be pursued without support and others that require mentor help – two models for challenge. This may be a simplification or a false dichotomy, as learning support can of course be provided in the form of written instructions and the ZPD requirements do not have to be filled by individual 'live' oral instruction, just as cognitive dissonance can often be best pursued by interaction with a questioning teacher.

However, the different concepts of learning provide a basis for contrasting approaches to classroom activities that could be useful in research that will inevitably entail a degree of imposition of false structures for the purposes of investigation. There is likely to be a place for both styles of challenge, but it would be interesting to see if one proves more satisfying than the other. From knowledge and experience of working with the highly able, I would expect children to demonstrate a slight preference for working alone, not for anti-social reasons, but to allow control over the pace of learning. Able pupils spend a great deal of time adjusting their rate of work to fit in with other class members and testify that they are relieved to be permitted to control their own learning (See Gallagher *et al*, 1997; Stanley, 1993; Suplee, 1990).

Detailed research into learning styles is another possible area for consideration and is already a common subject for psychological research. Focusing on the highly able child may help teachers when they are tailoring tasks to pupil preferences. Some workshop activities move at a tremendous pace, providing an overview of subjects and introducing a wealth of ideas. Others allow for in-depth study of a single complex idea and while some pupils are happy with both approaches, others firmly prefer either depth or breadth. It would be illuminating to find out the reasons for such preferences, whether subject areas, age groups, stage of schooling, or individual learning preferences.

The role of the teacher is possibly of equal importance to the subject matter and nature of task. I have cited several reports into pupils' preferred characteristics for their teachers, and this work could be expanded. Most studies have been undertaken in the USA and cultural difference could be evident if such an enquiry were replicated in the UK. Implications for learning assistants, parent helpers and mentor schemes could also be explored, leading to suggestions for restructuring school more around ability than age. This would impact on differentiation. If, for example, core subjects were taught entirely through flexible ability groups, teachers could minimise the potential social difficulties that can accompany acceleration, whilst providing pupils with activities at appropriate cognitive levels.

What of quantity of challenge? Children currently experiencing dissatisfaction which is becoming disaffection may be content with minimal attention even to one area of study. This may not be enough. Without investigation it is an important unanswered question that has direct implications for the cost of provision.

Why some subject areas are more appealing to the highly able is worth reviewing. One starting point could be an evaluation of enrichment activities, with an audit of provision that explicitly aims to challenge. Fields of study with underlying complexities, baffling questions and controversial issues are popular because of their potential for genuine research and as a rich source of engaging activities. Investigative and problem solving tasks are obviously popular with the highly able and most subjects can lend themselves to these approaches by planning activities carefully. The framing of questions is more important than the subject material itself and elaborate investigations can be undertaken with minimal resources.

The highly able achiever may be a different case. Sometimes pupils who achieve consistently high grades in traditionally taught subjects find open-ended tasks disconcerting. Embarking on a project with very little structure or no clear end point can be distressing to those who like clearly defined boundaries and this also merits exploration.

Similarly, the needs of the underachieving able merit more consideration, particularly in terms of the focus of provision. Dual aims of supporting children with problems and providing challenge are complex to satisfy. For many teachers, the first impulse would be to focus on remediating weakness and helping strengthen areas of difficulty, but a different tactic may be more effective. Research could discover the outcome of affording children the opportunity to pursue a challenging project of their choice, receiving only minimal support. In my experience, the learning problem becomes almost irrelevant as pupils who are fuelled by enthusiasm find alternative ways to express their findings. Research could confirm whether this is a generalisable phenomenon and whether the answer is positive or negative. Implications for SEN support follow.

Genuine potential for both success or failure is characteristic of challenge. It is inevitably disheartening to set off on a journey doomed to fail and just as empty to go through the motions of a simple task with an unimaginative and obvious conclusion. What constitutes challenge needs significant investigation and clarification if the entitlement of the highly able to equality of challenge is to be taken seriously.

Implications for teachers and policy makers

The research ideas outlined are relevant to teachers and policy makers, but they are long term and some aspects are unresolved. More immediate perspectives on the able are highlighted in this concluding section.

From the discussion and clarification of the language we use to discuss the able it is patent that care must be taken when discussing what we mean by intelligence and high ability. Readers should approach the gifted education literature with a critical eye and be clear that it is simplistic merely to equate high ability with high achievement and that any definition should incorporate people with learning problems, disabilities and cultural difference.

Concerning the issue of fairness and high ability, I have equipped readers with morally defensible arguments to support provision for the highly able. Through refining terms and identifying weaknesses in common criticisms of provision for the able, teachers and policy makers can advocate for the highly able. My contribution to the equality debate is the notion of providing equality of challenge, or equality of quality of learning, which is applicable to all children, even when this means provision is inegalitarian. Pupils should be allowed an education based on their needs and this would incorporate appropriate challenge.

Concerning provision, I emphasised the adoption of an inclusive approach that includes able underachievers. In reviewing the common approaches of acceleration, extension and enrichment, it is important to weigh up the effects on pupils, teachers and the wider school community. Schools need a flexible approach and the focus again is on ensuring that pupils are appropriately challenged (Reis and Westberg, 1994; Renzulli and Reis, 2003.

Since programmes of critical thinking skills could fill this requirement, they merit closer examination by educators. This examination should be undertaken with rigour and particularly where programmes are based on shaky theoretical foundations, their efficacy must be somehow verifiable in the particular context in which they will be used.

I suggested that the most promising programme for the highly able child is Philosophy with Children. Many of the objections to PwC are irrelevant for highly able children, but I am not presenting PwC as a panacea. It is a viable option, with sufficient flexibility and challenge to meet many of the requirements for a workable, practical response to the issue of provision for the able.

Since 'all educational policy decisions are political acts' (Rudnitski, 2000:673), it is vital that they are made with appropriate grounding and theoretical support. As teachers affect the lives of children every day, it is crucial that they have a clear idea about why they hold the attitudes they hold and why they use the teaching methods and resources they use, especially where significant choice is available. The able need advocates with strong arguments to counter the common knee jerk negativity they face. Things are improving, but not everywhere, and some children are still floundering.

> Certainly, there have been impressive gains in both research and educational practice; unfortunately there are only small pockets of this exemplary work being carried out. *Yewchuk and Lupart, 2000:666*

Highly able children merit a challenging educational experience and this can be promoted without resorting to elitist standpoints, even when provision outside the statutory curriculum is demanded. Their well being affects fellow pupils, parents, teachers and broader society. Ultimately we have too much to lose if these children feel disenfranchised, and everything to gain from ensuring that all children are engaged and motivated in their learning.

References

Adey, P. and Shayer, M. (1994) *Really Raising Standards* London: Routledge

Andrews, J.N. (1990) 'General Thinking Skills: are there such things?' in *Journal of Philosophy of Education* Vol. 24, No. 1, pp.71-9

Bailin, S. and Siegel, H. (2003) 'Critical Thinking' in Blake, N., Smeyers, P., Smith, R. and Standish, P. (eds) *The Blackwell Guide to Philosophy of Education* pp.181-192 Oxford: Blackwell

Bailin, S., Case, R., Coombs, J.R. and Daniels, L.B. (1999) 'Common misconceptions of critical thinking' in *Journal of Curriculum Studies* Vol. 31, No. 3, pp.269-83

Baldwin, A.Y., Vialle, W. and Clarke, C. (2000) 'Global Professionalism and Perceptions of Teachers of the Gifted' in Heller *et al* (eds), *op cit*

Bamberger, J. (1982) 'Cognitive Issues in the development of musically gifted children', in Sternberg, R.J. and Davidson, J. (eds) *Conceptions of Giftedness* New York: CUP pp.388-413

Baumfield, V. and Johnson, S. (2001) 'Ill thought out thinking skills' in *Teaching Thinking* winter pp.15-16

Benbow, C.P. and Stanley J.C. (1997). 'Inequity in equity: how equity can lead to inequity for high-potential students' in *Roeper Review* Vol.2, No.2, pp.249-92

Benn, C. and Chitty, C. 1999 'Myth: Educational Potential is a Fixed Quantity' in O'Hagan, B. (ed) *Modern Educational Myths: the future of democratic comprehensive education* London: Kogan Page pp.9-24

Best, R. (2000) 'Empathy, Experience and SMSC (Spiritual, Moral, Social and Cultural Education)' in *Pastoral Care*, December, pp8-18

Blagg, N., Ballinger, M. and Gardner, R. (1988) *Somerset Thinking Skills Course* Oxford: Blackwell

Blagg, N. and Ballinger, M. (1989) 'Somerset Thinking Skills Course' in Coles, M.J. and Robinson, W.D. (eds) *Teaching Thinking: A survey of Programmes in Education* Bristol: The Bristol Press pp.103-115

Bonnett, M. (1995) 'Teaching Thinking, and the Sanctity of Content' in *Journal of Philosophy of Education* Vol. 29, No. 3, pp.296-309

Borland, J.H. (1986) 'IQ Tests: throwing out the bathwater, saving the baby' in *Roeper Review* Vol. 8, No. 3, pp.163-7

151

Braggett, E.J. (1997) 'A developmental concept of giftedness: implications for the regular classroom' *Gifted Education International* Vol. 12, No. 2, pp.64-71

Brighouse, H. (2000) *School Choice and Social Justice* Oxford: Oxford University Press

Brighouse, H. (1995) 'In Defence of Educational Equality' in *Journal of Philosophy of Education* Vol. 29, No. 3, pp.416-420

Brighouse, H. (2002) 'Meritocracy and Educational Equality' from Seminar on Social Mobility and Meritocracy: Interdisciplinary perspectives on current issues, Nuffield College, Oxford University, February 16

Brody, N. (2000) 'History of Theories and Measurement of Intelligence' in Sternberg, R.J. (ed), *A Handbook of Intelligence* pp.16-33

Buzan, T. (1984) *Use Your Head* Middx: Penguin

Buzan, T. (2003) *Mind Maps for Kids* London: Harper Collins

Cam, P. (1995) *Thinking Together: Philosophical Inquiry for the Classroom* Sydney: Hale and Iremonger

Campbell, J.R., Wagner, H. and Walhberg, H.J. (2000) 'Academic Competitions and Programs Designed to Challenge the Exceptionally Talented', in Heller *et al* (eds) *op cit*, pp.523-35

Carroll, J.B. (1997) 'Psychometrics, Intelligence and Public Perception' in *Intelligence* No. 24, Vol. 1, pp.25-52

Challoner, J. (2000) *The Brain* London: Macmillan

Clark, C. and Callow, R. (1998) *Educating Able Children* London: NACE/Fulton

Colangelo, N. and Assouline, S.G. (2000) 'Counseling gifted students' in Heller *et al* (eds) *op cit*, pp.595-608

Coles, M.J. and Robinson, W.D. (eds) (1989) *Teaching Thinking: A survey of Programmes in Education* Bristol: The Bristol Press

Collins Dictionary (1999) London: Harper Collins

Cooper, D. (1980) *Illusions of Equality* London: Routledge

Costello, P.J.M. (2000) *Thinking Skills and Early Childhood Education* London: David Fulton

Dasen, P.R. (1977) *Piagetian Psychology: Cross-cultural contributions* New York: Gardner

De Bono, E. (1969) *The Mechanism of Mind* Middx: Penguin

De Bono, E. (1970) *The Dog-Exercising Machine* Middx: Penguin

De Bono, E. (1976) *Teaching Thinking* London: Maurice Temple Smith

De Bono, E. (1992) *Teach Your Child How to Think* London: Viking

De Bono, E. (1995) *Teach Yourself to Think* London: Viking

Delisle, J.R. (1994a) 'The top ten statements that should never again be made by advocates of gifted children' in *Gifted Child Today* Vol. 17, No.2, pp.34-42

Delisle, J.R. (1994b) 'Dealing with the stereotype of underachievement' in *Gifted Child Today*, Vol. 17, No.6, pp.20-1

Department for Education and Employment (1999) Raising Aspirations in the 21st Century: A speech by the Rt. Hon. David Blunkett, Secretary of State for Education and Employment London: DfEE

Department for Education and Science (1989) *Discipline in Schools: Report of the Committee of Enquiry* Chaired by Lord Elton London: The Stationery Office

Department for Education and Skills (2002) Social Market Foundation think-tank address by the Rt. Hon. Margaret Hodge, Minister for Higher Education). Taken from BBC online. Downloaded 15/04/02

Department for Education and Skills (2002) Institute for Mechanical Engineering address by the Rt. Hon. Estelle Morris, Secretary of State for Education. Taken from BBC online speech delivered 16/05/02

Donaldson, M (1978) *Children's Minds* Glasgow: Fontana

Edwards, J. (1991) 'Research work on the CoRT method' in Maclure, S. and Davies, P. (eds) *Learning to Think: Thinking to Learn* Oxford: Pergamon

Eyre, D. (1997) *Able Children in Ordinary Schools* London: David Fulton

Eysenck, H.J. (1998) *Intelligence: a new look* New Jersey: Transaction Publishers

Feather, N.T. (1989) 'Attitudes towards the high achiever: the fall of the tall poppy' in *Australian Journal of Psychology* Vol. 41, No. 3, pp.239-67

Feldhusen, J.F. and Jarwan F.A. (2000) 'Identification of gifted and talented youth for educational programs' in Heller *et al* (eds) *op cit,* pp.271-82

Feldhusen, J.F. (1996) 'Talent as an alternative conception of giftedness' in *Gifted Education International* Vol. 11, No. 3, pp.124-7

Feldman, D.H. and Goldsmith L.T. (1986) *Nature's Gambit* New York: Basic Books

Feuerstein, R., Rand, Y., Hoffman, M.B. and Miller, R. (1980) *Instrumental Enrichment: an intervention programme for cognitive modifiability* Baltimore: Uni Park Press

Fisher, E. (1981) 'The effect of labelling on gifted children and their families' in *Roeper Review* Vol. 3, No.3 pp.37-44

Fisher, R. (1990) *Teaching Children to Think* London: Blackwell

Fisher, R. (1997) *Poems for Thinking* Oxford: Nash Pollock

Fisher, R. (1998) *Teaching Thinking* London: Cassell

Fisher, R. (2003) 'Kid's stuff?' in *The Philosopher's Magazine* Issue 24, Vol.4, pp.33,34,37

Freeman, J. (1983) 'Emotional Problems of the Gifted Child' in *Journal of Child Psychology and Psychiatry and Allied Disciplines* Vol. 24, No. 3, pp.481-5

Freeman, J. (1990) *Gifted Children Growing Up* London: Cassell

Freeman, J. (1997) 'The emotional development of the highly able' in *European Journal of Psychology of Education* Vol. 12, No. 4, pp.479-93

Freeman, J. (1998) *Educating the Very Able: Current International Research* London: The Stationery Office

Freeman, J. (2000) 'Families: the Essential Context for Gifts and Talents' in Heller *et al* (eds) *op cit,* pp.694-705

Freeman, J. (2001) *Gifted Children Grown Up*. London: David Fulton

Gagné, F. (1997) 'Critique of Morelock's (1996) definitions of giftedness and talent' *Roeper Review* Vol. 20, No. 2, pp.76-85

Gagné, F. (1998) 'A proposal for subcategories within gifted or talented populations' in *Gifted Child Quarterly* Vol. 42, No. 2, pp.87-95

Gagné, F. (2000) 'Understanding the Complex Choreography of Talent Development Through DMGT-Based Analysis' in Heller *et al* (eds) *op cit*, pp.67-80

Gallagher, J.J., Harradine, C.C. and Coleman, M.R. (1997) 'Challenge or Boredom? gifted students' views on their schooling' *Roeper Review* Vol. 19., No. 3, pp.132-6

Gallagher, J.J. (2000) 'Changing Paradigms for Gifted Education in the United States' in Heller *et al* (eds) *op cit* pp.681-94

Galton, F. (1865) Hereditary Intelligence: An inquiry into its laws and consequences *MacMillan's Magazine*, Vol.2, pp.157-66

Gardner, H. (1983) *Frames of Mind: the Theory of Multiple Intelligences* NY: Basic Books

Gardner, H. (1999) *Intelligence Reframed* NY: Basic Books

Garner, P. (1999) *Pupils with Problems* Staffs: Trentham Books

Gazzard, A. (1989) 'Philosophy for Children and the Piagetian Framework' in *Thinking: The Journal of Philosophy for Children* Vol. 5, No. 1, pp.10-14

Gazzard. A. (1996) 'Philosophy for Children and the Discipline of Philosophy' in *Thinking: The Journal of Philosophy for Children* Vol. 12, No. 4, pp.26-31

George, D. (1992) *The Challenge of the Able Child* London: Fulton

Goddard, A. 'Blair attacks 'cosy elitism of opponents of access targets' in *Times Higher Education Supplement* 20 March 2002, p3.

Goodhew, G. (2002) 'Gifted and Talented Programmes: are they working?' in *Special Children* March p26

Gottfredson, L.S. (1997) Mainstream science on intelligence: an editorail with 52 signatories, history and biography. *Intelligence*, Vol.24, No.1, pp.13-23

Grigorenko, E.L. (2000) 'Russian Gifted Education in Technical Disciplines' in Heller *et al* (eds) *op cit*, pp.735-42

Gross, M.U.M. (1993) *Exceptionally Gifted Children* London: Routledge

Gross, M.U.M. (1999) 'Small poppies: highly gifted children in the early years' in *Roeper Review* Vol. 20, No. 3

Gross, M.U.M. (2000) 'Issues in the Cognitive Development of Exceptionally and Profoundly Gifted in Heller *et al* (eds) *op cit*, pp.179-192

Hamlyn, D. (1967) in Peters, R.S. (ed) *The Concept of Education* London: Routledge Kegan Paul

Hannah, L.C. and Shore, B.M. (1995) 'Metacognition and High Intellectual Ability: insights from the study of learning-disabled gifted students' in *Gifted Child Quarterly* Vol. 39, No. 2, Spring, pp.95-109

Haroutunian-Gordon, S. (1998) 'Some issues in the critical thinking debate: dead horses and red herrings anyone?' in *Educational Theory* Vol. 48, No. 3, pp.411-24

Haynes, J. (2002) *Children as Philosophers* London: Routledge

Head, G. and O'Neill, W. (1999) 'Introducing Feuerstein's Instrumental Enrichment in a school for children with social, emotional and behavioural difficulties' in *Support for Learning* Vol. 14, No. 3, pp.122-128

Hellawell, D. (2002) 'The Fall of the Meritocracy: a response to Roy Hattersley' in *Education and Social Justice* Vol. 4.2, pp.33-36

Heller, K.A. and Schofield N.J. (2000) 'International Trends and Topics of Research on Giftedness and Talent' in Heller *et al* (eds) *op cit*, pp.123-40

Heller, K.A., Monks, F.J., Sternberg, R.J. and Subotnik, R.F. (eds) (2000) *International Handbook of Research and Development of Giftedness and Talent* Oxford: Elsevier Science

Herrnstein, R. J. and Murray, C. (1994) *The Bell Curve: Intelligence and class structure in American life* NY: Times Books

Higgins, S. and Baumfield, V. (1998) 'A Defence of Teaching General Thinking Skills' in *Journal of Philosophy of Education* Vol. 32, No. 3, pp 391-398

Howe, M.J.A. (1988) 'Intelligence as an explanation' in *British Journal of Psychology* Vol. 79, pp.349-60

Howe, M.J.A. (1990a) *The Origins of Exceptional Abilities* Oxford: Blackwell

Howe, M.J.A. (1990b) 'Children's Differing Capabilities: Doubts about common sense explanations' in *Gifted and Talented* No.1, Summer pp.28-31

Howe, M.J.A. (1997) *IQ in Question: The Truth About Intelligence* London: Sage

Hunsaker, S.L. (1994) 'Creativity as Characteristic of Giftedness: teachers see it, then they don't' in *Roeper Review* Vol. 17, No.1, pp.11-15

Illich, I. (1971) *Deschooling Society* Middx: Penguin

Institute for the Advancement of Philosophy for Children (1988) 'Philosophy for Children: Where we are now' in *Thinking: The Journal of Philosophy for Children Supplements* 1 and 2

Iveson, J. and Hallam, S. (2001) *Ability Grouping in Education* London: Paul Chapman

Jausovec, N. (1997) 'Differences in EEG alpha activity between gifted and non-identified individuals: insights into problem solving' *Gifted Child Quarterly* Vol. 11, No.1, pp.26-31

Jausovec, N. (2000) 'Differences in Cognitive Processes Between Gifted, Intelligent, Creative and Average Individuals While Solving Complex Problems: An EEG Study', in *Intelligence* No. 28, Vol. 3, pp.213-237

Johnson, S. (2001) *Teaching Thinking Skills* (Impact No. 8) Hants: PESGB

Johnson, S. and Gardner, P. (1999) 'Some Achilles' Heels of Thinking Skills: a response to Higgins and Baumfield' in *Journal of Philosophy of Education* Vol. 33, No. 3, pp 435-449

Jones, N. and Jones, B. (eds) (1992) *Learning to Behave: Curriculum and whole school management approaches to discipline* London: Kogan Page

Keating, D.P. (1975) 'Precocious cognitive development at the level of formal operations' in *Child Development Issue* 46, pp.276-280

Kellmer-Pringle, M. (1970) *Able Misfits: The educational and behaviour difficulties of intelligent children* London: Longman

Kerr, B., Colangelo, N. and Gaeth, J. (1988) 'Gifted adolescents' attitudes towards their giftedness' in *Gifted Child Quarterly* Vol. 32, No. 2, pp.245-7

Khatena, J. (1992) *Gifted: challenge and response for education* Chicago: F.E. Peacock

Kitchener, R (1990) 'Do children think philosophically?' in *Metaphilosophy*, Vol.21, No.4, pp.424-429

Kohan, W. (1998) 'What can philosophy and children offer each other?' in *Thinking: The Journal of Philosophy for Children* Vol. 14, No. 4, pp.2-8

Kornhaber, M. (1999) Enhancing Equity in Gifted Education: a framework for examining assessments drawing on the theory of multiple intelligence, in *High Ability Studies* Vol.10, No.2 pp.143-161

Koshy, V. and Casey, R (1996) *Effective Provision for Able and Exceptionally Able Children* London: Hodder and Stoughton

Koshy, V. and Casey, R (1998) 'A National Curriculum and the Sovreignty of Higher Ability Learners' in *Gifted Child Quarterly* Vol. 42, No. 4, Fall, pp.253-60

Lee-Corbin, H. and Denicolo, P. (1998) *Recognising and Supporting Able Children in Primary Schools* London: David Fulton

Leroux, J.A. (2000a) 'A Study of Education for High Ability Students in Canada: Policy, Programs and Student Needs' in Heller *et al* (eds) *op cit*, pp. 695-701

Leroux, J.A. (2000b) 'Shaping my life – evolving strategies of high-ability women' in Montgomery, D. *Able Underachievers* London: Whurr Publishers pp.191-201

Leyden, S. (1998) *Supporting the Child of Exceptional Ability at Home and School* London: David Fulton

Lipman, M. (1988) *Philosophy Goes to School* Philadephia: Temple University Press

Lipman, M. (1991) *Thinking in Education* Cambridge: Cambridge University Press

Lloyd, J. *Wall St Journal* 8/7/96 Vol.228, No.27 pA12

Machado, L.A. (1978) *El Derecho a ser Intelligente (The Right to be Intelligent)* Editorial *Seix Barral* Oxford: Pergamon

Maclure, S. and Davies, P. (eds) (1991) *Learning to Think: Thinking to Learn* Oxford, Pergamon

Matthews, G.B. (1978) 'The child as natural philosopher' in Lipman, M. and Sharp, A.M. (eds) *Growing up with Philosophy* Philadelphia: Temple University Press

Matthews, G.B. (1984) *Dialogues with Children* Cambridge: Harvard University Press

McAlpine, D. (1996) 'Who are the gifted and talented?: concepts and definitions' in *Gifted and Talented: New Zealand perspectives* McAlpine, D. and Moltzen, R. (eds) Palmerston: ERDC Press

McGuinness, C. (1999) From Thinking Skills to Thinking Classrooms: A review and evaluation of approaches for developing children's thinking *Research Brief* No.115 London: DfEE/HMSO

McPeck, J. (1981) *Critical Thinking and Education* Oxford: Martin Robertson

Monks, F.J., Heller, K.A. and Passow, H. (2000) 'The Study of Giftedness: Reflections on Where We Are and Where We Are Going' in Heller *et al* (eds) *op cit*, pp.839-863

Monks, F.J. and Mason, E.J. (2000) 'Developmental Psychology and Giftedness: Theories and Research' in Heller *et al* (eds) *op cit*, pp.141-56

Montgomery, D. (1996) *Educating the Able* London: Cassell

Montgomery, D. (2000) *Able Underachievers* London: Whurr Publishers

Montgomery, D (ed) (2003) *Gifted and Talented Children with Special Educational Needs* London: NACE/Fulton

Moon, S.M. and Rosselli, H.C. (2000) 'Developing gifted programs' in Heller *et al* (eds) *op cit*, pp.499-521

Morelock, M.J. and Feldman, D.H. (2000) 'Prodigies, Savants and Williams Syndrome: Windows Into Talent and Cognition' in Heller *et al* (eds) *op cit*, pp.227-41

Murris, K. (2000) 'Can 'Children Do Philosophy?' in *Journal of Philosophy of Education*, Vol. 34, No. 2, pp.46-52

Murris, K. (2001) 'Are children natural philosophers?' in *Teaching Thinking* Autumn pp.46-9

Ofsted (2001 – December) *Providing for gifted and talented pupils: An evaluation of Excellence in Cities and other grant funded programmes* London: Ofsted

Pagnin, A. and Andreani, O.D. (2000) 'New trends in research on moral development in the gifted programs' in Heller *et al* (eds) *op cit*, pp.467-84

Persson, R.S., Joswig, H. and Balogh, L. (2000) 'Europe: Programs, Practices, and Current Research' in Heller *et al* (eds) *op cit*, pp.703-34

Plomin, R. (1998) 'The genetics of cognitive abilities and disabilities' in *Scientific American*, May, pp.62-9

Plucker, J.A., Callahan, C.M. and Tomchin, F. (1996) 'Wherefore art thou multiple intelligences? alternative assessments for identifying talent in ethnically diverse and low income students' in *Gifted Child Quarterly* Vol. 40., No. 1., pp.81-92

Porter, L. (1999) *Gifted Young Children: A Guide for Teachers and Parents* Buckingham: OUP

Quinn, V. (1994) 'A Defence of Critical Thinking as a Subject: if McPeck is wrong he is wrong' in *Journal of Philosophy of Education* Vol. 28, No.1, pp.101-11

Radford, J. (1990) *Child Prodigies and Exceptionally Early Achievers* New York: Free Press

Radford, J. (1998) 'Prodigies in the Press' in *High Ability Studies*, vol.9, No.2 pp.153-164

Reis, S.M. and Westberg, K.L. (1994) 'The impact of staff development on teachers' ability to modify curriculum for gifted and talented students' *Gifted Child Quarterly* Vol. 38, No. 3., pp.127-35

Renzulli, J.S. (1982) What makes a problem real: Stalking the illusive meaning of qualitative differences in gifted education' in *Gifted Child Quarterly*, Vol.26, 147-156

Renzulli, J.S. and Reis, S.M. (2000) 'The Schoolwide Enrichment Model' in Heller *et al* (eds) *op cit*, pp.367-81

Renzulli, J.S. and Reis, S.M. (2003) 'Research related to the Schoolwide Enrichment Triad Model' in *Gifted Education International* Vol. 18, pp.15-39

Richardson, K. (1991) *Understanding Intelligence* Bucks:OUP

Rudnitski, R.A. (2000) 'National/Provincial Gifted Education Policies: Present State, Future Possibilities' in Heller *et al* (eds) *op cit*, pp.673-79

Scheffler, I. (1985) 'On Human Potential: an essay in the philosophy of education' reviewed by White, J. (1986) 'On Reconstructing the Concept of Human Potential' *Journal of Philosophy of Education*, Vol. 20, No. 1, pp 133-142.

Schoon, I. (2000) 'A Life Span Approach to Talent' in Heller *et al* (eds) *op cit*, pp.213-225

Sharron, H. (2001) Diagnosing learning difficulties in *Teaching Thinking* Summer pp.32-37

Shayer, M. and Adey, P. (eds) (2002) *Learning Intelligence: Cognitive acceleration across the curriculum from 5-15 years* Bucks: Open University Press

Shi, J. and Zha, Z. (2000) 'Psychological Research on and Education of Gifted and Talented Children in China' in Heller *et al* (eds) *op cit*, pp.757-63

Shutter-Dyson, R. and Gabriel, C. (1986) 'Musical Giftedness' in Freeman, J. (ed) *The Psychology of Gifted Children* pp159-183 Chichester: Wiley

Siegel, H. (1988) *Educating Reason: Rationality, Critical Thinking and Education* New York: Routledge

Simonton, D. K. (2000) 'Genius and Giftedness: Same or Different? in Heller *et al* (eds) *op cit*, pp.111-21

Smutny, J.E., Walker, S.Y. and Meckstroth, E.A. (1997) *Teaching Young Gifted Children in the Classroom: identifying, nurturing and challenging ages 4-9* Minneapolis: Free Spirit

Soriano de Alencar, E.M.L., Blumen-Pardo, S. and Castellanos-Simons, D. (2000) 'Programs and Practices for Identifying and Nurturing Giftedness and Talent in Latin American Countries' in Heller *et al* (eds) *op cit*, pp.817-29

Stanley, J.C. (1993) 'Gifted children and the zone of proximal development' in *Gifted Education International*, Vol. 9 pp.78-81.

Sternberg, R.J. (1990) *Metaphors of Mind* Cambridge: Cambridge University Press

Sternberg, R.J. (1996) 'Neither elitism nor egalitarianism: gifted education as a third force in American education' in *Roeper Review* Vol. 18, No. 3, p.143-7

Sternberg, R.J. (ed) (2000) *Handbook of Intelligence* Cambridge: Cambridge University Press

Suplee, P.L. (1990) *Reaching the Gifted Underachiever: program strategy and design* NY: Teachers College Press

Sutherland, P. (1992) *Cognitive Development Today: Piaget and his critics* London: Paul Chapman

Swift, A. (2001) *Political Philosophy: A beginners' guide for Students and Politicians* Cambridge: Polity

Tannenbaum, A.J. (1983) *Gifted Children: psychological and educational perspectives* New York: MacMillan

Tannenbaum, A.J. (2000a) 'A History of Giftedness in School and Society' in Heller *et al* (eds) *op cit,* pp.23-53

Tannenbaum, A.J. (2000b) 'Giftedness: the Ultimate Instrument for Good and Evil' in Heller *et al* (eds) *op cit,* pp.447-65

Taylor, C. and Kokot, S. (2000) 'The Status of Gifted Child Education in Africa' in Heller *et al* (eds) *op cit,* pp.799-815

Tizard, B. and Hughes, M. (1990) 'The four-year-old thinker' in *Thinking: The Journal of Philosophy for Children* Vol. 6, No. 5, pp.17-21

Tooley, J. (2000) *Reclaiming Education* London: Cassell

Tucker, B. and Hafenstein, N.L. (1997) 'Psychological intensities in young gifted children' *Gifted Child Quarterly* Vol. 41, No.3, pp.66-75

Turgeon, W. (1998) 'Metaphysical Horizons of Philosophy for Children: A survey of recent discussion within the philosophy for children community' in *Thinking: The Journal of Philosophy for Children* Vol. 14, No. 2, pp.18-22

Van Tassel-Baska, J. (2001) 'The talent development process: what we know and what we don't know' in *Gifted Education International* Vol. 16, pp.20-28

Van Tassel-Baska, J., Johnson, D. and Avery, L.D. (2002) 'Using performance tasks in the identification of economically disadvantaged and minority gifted learners: findings from Project STAR' in *Gifted Child Quarterly* Vol. 46, No. 2, Spring, pp.110-123

Vygotsky, L.S. (1986) *Thought and Language* Mass: Harvard University Press

Waldren, J. (for the QCA) (2003) 'World Class Arena: providing an international perspective on assessing gifted and talented students' in *Gifted Education International* Vol. 17, pp.139-44

Wallace, B. (2000) *Teaching the Very Able Child* London: NACE/Fulton

Ward, L. (2003) 'Gifted pupils' scheme has little impact in classroom, says schools inspector' in *The Guardian* 23-12-03

Watts, G. 2002 'A Bunch of Jolly Good Fellows or Old Cronies Who Don't Deserve £25m a Year? in *Times Higher Education Supplement* 05/04/02, Issue No. 1532, pp.18-19

Webb, R.A. (1974) 'Concrete and formal operations in very bright 6 to 11 year olds' in *Human Development* 17, pp.292-300

Westwood, P.S. (2001) 'Differentiation as a strategy for inclusive classroom practice: some difficulties identified' in *Australian Journal of Learning Disabilities,* Vol.6, No.1 pp.5-61

Westwood, P.S. (2003) *Commonsense Methods for Children with Special Educational Needs* London, Routledge Falmer

Whalley, M.J. (1987) 'Unexamined lives: the case for philosophy in schools' in *British Journal of Educational Studies,* Vol.35, No.3, pp.260-80

White, C.S. (1985) 'Alternatives for assessing the presence of advanced intellectual abilities in young children' *Roeper Review* Vol. 8, No. 2, pp.73-5

White, J.P. (1992) 'The roots of philosophy', in Griffiths, A.P. (ed), *The Impulse to Philosophise* Cambridge: Cambridge University Press pp.73-88

White, J.P. (1994) 'The Dishwasher's Child: education and the end of egalitarianism' in *Journal of the Philosophy of Education* Vol. 28 No. 2 pp.180-192

White, J.P. (2002) *The Child's Mind* London: Routledge

White, J. and White, P. (1980) 'David Cooper's Illusions' in *Journal of Philosophy of Education* Vol. 14, No. 2, pp.239-248

White, J.P. (1974) 'Intelligence and the Logic of the Nature-Nurture Issue' in *Journal of the Philosophy of Education* Vol. 3, No.1, pp.30-51

Whitmore, J.R. (1986) 'Understanding a lack of motivation to excel' in *Gifted Child Quarterly* Vol. 30, No. 2, pp.66-9

Williams, M. (2003) 'The importance of metacognition in the literacy development of young gifted and talented children' in *Gifted Educational International* Vol. 17, pp.249-58

Winch, C. (1988) 'Ability, Intelligence and Practical Education' in *Journal of Philosophy of Education* Vol. 22, No. 1, pp.35-42

Winch, C (1990) *Language, Ability and Educational Achievement* London: Routledge

Winch, C. (1996) 'Equality, Quality and Diversity' Ch. 10 in special edition of *Journal of Philosophy of Education* Vol. 30, No. 1, pp.113-128

Winch, C. and Gingell, J. (1999) *Dictionary of Philosophy of Education* London: Routledge

Winner, E. and Martino, G. (2000) 'Giftedness in Non-Academic Domains: the Case of the Visual Arts and Music' in Heller *et al* (eds) *op cit*, pp.95-109

Winstanley, C.J. (2003) 'Highly able children with hearing impairments' in Montgomery, D (ed) *Gifted and Talented Children with Special Educational Needs* London: NACE / Fulton

Wollam, J. (1992) 'Equality versus excellence – the South Korean dilemma in gifted education' in *Roeper Review* Vol. 14, No. 4, pp.37-43

Wu, W.T., Cho, S. and Munandar, U. (2000) 'Programs and Practices for Identifying and Nurturing Giftedness and Talent in Asia (outside mainland China)' in Heller *et al* (eds) *op cit*, pp.765-778

Yewchuk, C. and Lupart, J. (2000) 'Inclusive Education for Gifted Students with Disabilities', in Heller *et al* (eds) *International Handbook of Research and Development of Giftedness and Talent* Oxford: Elsevier Science pp.659-672

Yewchuk, C. (1995) 'The 'mad genius' controversy: implications for gifted education' in *Journal for Education of the Gifted* Vol. 19, No. 1, pp.3-29

Ziegler, A. and Heller, K.A. (2000) 'Conceptions of Giftedness from a Meta-Theoretical Perspective' in Heller *et al* (eds) *op cit*, pp.3-22

Ziegler, A. and Raul, T. (2000) 'Myth and Reality: a review of empirical studies on giftedness' in *High Ability Studies* Vol. 11, No. 2, pp.113-136

Internet sites

www.dfes.gov.uk www.giftltd.co.uk
www.nace.co.uk www.nagcbritain.org.uk
www.worldgifted.org

Index